SECRETS

IN

HIGH PLACES

I dedicate this book to Lynn, Katharine, Ashley and Celia for their infinite patience and love.

I wish to thank Kitson Vincent for his steadfast vision and John Wood for sage advice. Their contributions made this project a reality.

I thank all my teammates for their enthusiasm and hard work.

I would like to thank everyone at the Breakout Educational Network/Stornoway Productions — Paul, Inta, Criss, Alex, Wilma and Jude — for their help on this project. Finally, I want to recognize the excellent editing job done by Amanda Stewart at First Folio.

Jay Innes
Fall 2002

SECRETS

IN

HIGH PLACES

BY

JAY INNES

BREAKOUT EDUCATIONAL NETWORK
IN ASSOCIATION WITH
DUNDURN PRESS
TORONTO · OXFORD

Copyright © Breakout Educational Network, 2003

www.breakout-ed.net

Publisher: Inta D. Erwin
Editor: Amanda Stewart, First Folio Resource Group
Designer: Bruna Brunelli, Brunelli Designs
Printer: Webcom

National Library of Canada Cataloguing in Publication Data

Innes, Jay
  Secrets in high places/by Jay Innes

One of the 16 vols. and 14 hours of video which make up the
  underground royal commission report.
Includes bibliographical references and index.
ISBN 1-55002-423-X

  1. Government spending policy — Canada. 2. Canada —
Appropriations and expenditures. I. Title. II. Title: underground
royal commission report.

HJ9921.I55 2003   336.3'9'0971   C2003-902303-3

1   2   3   4   5   07   06   05   04   03

Printed and bound in Canada.
Printed on recycled paper. ❀
www.dundurn.com

Exclusive Canadian broadcast rights for the *underground royal commission* report

Check your cable or satellite listings for telecast times.

Visit the *urc* Web site link at:
www.ichanneltv.com

About the *underground royal commission* Report

Since September 11, 2001, there has been an uneasy dialogue among Canadians as we ponder our position in the world, especially vis à vis the United States. Critically and painfully, we are re-examining ourselves and our government. We are even questioning our nation's ability to retain its sovereignty.

The questions we are asking ourselves are not new. Over the last 30 years, and especially in the dreadful period of the early 1990s, leading up to the Quebec referendum of 1995, inquiries and royal commissions, one after another, studied the state of the country. What *is* new is that eight years ago, a group of citizens looked at this parade of inquiries and commissions and said, "These don't deal with the real issues." They wondered how it was possible for a nation that was so promising and prosperous in the early 1960s to end up so confused, divided and troubled. And they decided that what was needed was a different kind of investigation — driven from the grassroots "bottom," and not from the top. Almost as a provocation, this group of people, most of whom were affiliated with the award-winning documentary-maker Stornoway Productions, decided to do it themselves — and so was born the *underground royal commission*!

What began as a television documentary soon evolved into much more. Seven young, novice researchers, hired right out of university, along with a television crew and producer, conducted interviews with people in government, business, the military and in all walks of life, across the country. What they discovered went beyond anything they had expected. The more they learned, the larger the implications grew. The project continued to evolve and has expanded to include a total of 23 researchers over the last several years. The results are the 14 hours of video and 16 books that make up the first interim report of the *underground royal commission*.

So what *are* the issues? The report of the *underground royal commission* clearly shows us that regardless of region, level of government or political party, we are operating under a wasteful system ubiquitously lacking in accountability. An ever-weakening connection between the electors and the elected means that we are slowly and irrevocably losing our right to know our government. The researchers' experiences demonstrate that it is almost impossible for a member of the public, or in most cases even for a member of Parliament, to actually trace how our tax dollars are spent. Most disturbing is the fact that our young people have been stuck with a crippling IOU that has effectively hamstrung their future. No wonder, then, that Canada is not poised for reaching its potential in the 21st century.

The *underground royal commission* report, prepared in large part by and for the youth of Canada, provides the hard evidence of the problems you and I may long have suspected. Some of that evidence makes it clear that, as ordinary Canadians, we are every bit as culpable as our politicians — for our failure to demand accountability, for our easy acceptance of government subsidies and services established without proper funding in place, and for the disservice we have done to our young people through the debt we have so blithely passed on to them. But the real purpose of the *underground royal commission* is to ensure that we better understand how government processes work and what role we play in them. Public policy issues must be understandable and accessible to the public if they are ever to be truly addressed and resolved. The *underground royal commission* intends to continue pointing the way for bringing about constructive change in Canada.

— Stornoway Productions

Books in the *underground royal commission* Report

"Just Trust Us"

The Chatter Box
The Chance of War
Talking Heads Talking Arms: (3 volumes)
No Life Jackets
Whistling Past the Graveyard
Playing the Ostrich

Days of Reckoning
Taking or Making Wealth
Guardians on Trial
Goodbye Canada?
Down the Road Never Travelled
Secrets in High Places
On the Money Trail

Does Your Vote Count?
A Call to Account
Reflections on Canadian Character

Fourteen hours of videos are also available with the *underground royal commission* report.
Visit Stornoway Productions at www.stornoway.com for a list of titles.

TABLE OF CONTENTS

PREFACE

Jay Innes has done Canada, Canadians, our political leaders and public servants a great service. He and his team of researchers document in this book their trials and tribulations in their attempts to secure answers about an important government program, the Canada Infrastructure Works Program. That the program involved the three levels of government — federal, provincial and municipal — is an added bonus because it gives the reader a window on how intergovernmental relations in Canada actually work at the program-delivery level.

There are several important messages in this book for anyone interested in how governments operate and make decisions. It reveals the daunting challenge an individual would face if he or she set out to secure answers about the application of a government program. It demonstrates how difficult it is for government to establish the success of its programs. It speaks to what motivates politicians and career officials in their work. It is essential reading for all those who want to understand government and improve our system of governance.

Secrets in High Places also raises several important questions that require reflection. Why is it that many career officials provide vague answers, avoid making firm commitments and choose not to return telephone calls? Why is it that politicians value visibility above many other things? Why do so many public servants need to sit on intergovernmental committees? How can we properly define what belongs in a ministerial office and what belongs to career officials and government departments? In short, not only has Jay Innes shed light on how government functions, he has also provided a research agenda for journalists, academics, politicians, public servants and, above all, Canadians to pursue.

Donald J. Savoie
Holder of the Clément-Cormier Chair in Economic Development
at the Université de Moncton, New Brunswick
October 2002

"You know about the infrastructure program? It's a co-operative effort.

"I love it when governments get together on something: 'OK, tell you what, we the feds will put in some money, the provinces will put in their money and the municipalities will kick in theirs.'

"So as a taxpayer, I'm goin', 'OK, I'll put in some money, then I'll add some money to that, and I'll add some more money to that.'"

Glen Foster, comedian

INTRODUCTION

After eight years working for Stornoway Productions, two federal elections and hundreds of interviews with politicians and public servants, I thought I had exhausted my ability to be surprised. I now find out that I'm wrong — a rare admission when dealing with modern-day politics.

I'll explain. One recent spring morning I opened up the *Ottawa Citizen* to read that one of the banks had commissioned a study on the future of Canadian cities. The study concluded that the country's municipal infrastructure needed $44 billion in repairs.[1]

That $44-billion figure sounded so familiar. I remembered a 1996 report I had read on the state of the nation's infrastructure, conducted by a professor at McGill University. I dug out the report and began to reread it. Sure enough, there was that number again. The McGill report estimated that an update of our decaying infrastructure would cost every Canadian $1,500 — a tidy sum of $44 billion total.

I was surprised that a current report had come to the same conclusion as one written many years earlier, in the mid-1990s, because between 1993 and 1999 the federal government, together with the provinces and the municipalities, had spent a total of $8.3 billion under a national infrastructure program to fund 17,000 projects.

Why had the government's infrastructure program failed to make even a dent in the $44-billion estimate of 1996? Did the new report consider depreciation or factor in projects that were neglected in the earlier study? Whatever the reason, I realized, as I mused over the article, that it was just these sorts of questions — and the desire to follow up on government promises — that had served as the impetus for this book.

The case studies found in the chapters that follow began with the hunt to specifically identify a few of the promises attached to the government's infrastructure projects. Once the promises had been identified, the next logical question was, did the program deliver on these promises? Was infrastructure money responsible for keeping the NHL's Calgary Flames in Canada? Was the "one-time" subsidy enough to restore a 70-year-old theatre to its past glory? Did it prevent a professional tennis tournament from leaving Montreal? Most importantly, were these objectives consistent with the original overall goals of the infrastructure program?

As I and my research team searched for the answers to these questions, we found example after example of promises and objectives that had been altered, or even changed altogether. And that's when it hit home: these ever-changing promises have repercussions for citizens who want to participate in our system of responsible government. As citizens we have a right — and a duty — to ask questions about the way our tax dollars are spent. But if we are to do our part and hold the people we elect to account for their actions, we need government to design programs with clear objectives, transparent decision-making processes and well-defined methods for monitoring and assessing outcomes.

I still haven't figured out why the cost to repair the country's infrastructure is the same in 2002 as it was in 1996. The answer, I suspect, lies somewhere in the tangled and complicated relationship that connects the needs of the citizens, government promises and program results.

Jay Innes
November 2002

NOTES

1. Mohammed Adam, "Let cities tax more, bank says," *Ottawa Citizen*, April 23, 2002, pp. A1, A10.

PART I

The Politics of Plumbing

"Nobody was ever re-elected by promising better plumbing."

Tom McMillan, then minister of the environment,
at the First Canadian Conference on Urban Infrastructure,
February, 1987[1]

CHAPTER 1

The Journey Begins

This is the story of one citizen who tried to understand how his government works.

In 1997 I decided to study the Canada Infrastructure Works Program (CIWP), a cost-shared program paid for equally by the federal, provincial and municipal governments. The program began in early 1994 and when it finally ended in the spring of 1999, more than $8.3 billion had been spent on 17,000 infrastructure projects across the country.

When I convinced Toronto's Stornoway Productions to let me document the program in preparation for a television series, I assumed the job wouldn't take more than a summer. I also assumed that the word "infrastructure" referred to roads, sewers and bridges.

I made a lot of wrong assumptions in those days.

I should have suspected that the job would be tougher than first imagined because I wasn't exactly a neophyte when it came to examining government spending.

Let me explain.

Stornoway Productions hired me in the fall of 1994, when the country seemed to be coming unstuck. The continuous string of federal government deficits and the mushrooming national debt were attracting attention beyond our borders. In early 1995 the influential *Wall Street Journal* editorial writers had questioned whether Canada was bankrupt, comparing the nation to Third World countries that are unable to manage their debts. The unemployment rate was stuck in double digits and public despair over the lack of job prospects was great — as evidenced by the thousands of people who lined up for several days in January outside a Toronto-area convention centre in hopes of landing a job with a local car manufacturer. Meanwhile public anger and cynicism with government was manifesting itself in regional discontent. The Reform Party was attracting attention in the West; the Quebec separatist movement was regaining momentum; and tax rallies attended by angry citizens were making the morning news.

Around this time Stornoway was planning to shoot a documentary series called *Days of Reckoning*. I was hired to be part of a team of seven young Canadians, all fresh out of university, who would attempt to find out how a country that was so proud and prosperous in its centennial year — about the time that many of us were born — could end up debt-ridden and divided just 30 years later. While much of the work to understand the debt might have been done sitting in a Toronto office researching government policies and trying to understand the impact of compound interest, we determined that the process of collecting information would be as important as the discoveries. Our approach would be hands-on. Through trial and error we would draw conclusions as they emerged from our own experiences.

To gain a broad Canadian perspective, we crossed the country to talk to people from a variety of backgrounds. For months we travelled by plane, train, ferry and van, interviewing more than 130 people in 10 provinces, from former politicians and public servants to New Brunswick lumbermen, Saskatchewan pig farmers, Alberta oilmen and Quebec lawyers.

During our journey we all acquired a better knowledge of the national debt, as well as an understanding of the attitudes and practices that permitted it to grow unchecked for over 30 years. We found out just how pervasive government programs and subsidies were across the country. In interview after interview, example after example, we heard about billions of dollars that were spread about the land and wasted, apparently with no strings attached, because there wasn't any threat of consequence. We found government funding business ventures using loan guarantees (which are really subsidies because it is the taxpayer who picks up the tab when a government-backed venture fails). In fact, we discovered that subsidies had infiltrated almost every facet of our lives, to the extent that an industry of lobbyists and consultants had sprung up to help Canadians find the quickest route to access such funding. The prevalence of subsidies and free money had conditioned our behaviour, and as a result whole regions of the country had become dependent on handouts.

We were told that governments don't make decisions the way ordinary citizens and the private sector do, that is, considering all the options before spending money. We found examples where governments had never weighed the costs and benefits or factored in the opportunity costs of particular spending decisions.

When former auditor general Kenneth Dye spoke with us, however, he made it clear that the national debt did indeed have an enormous opportunity cost attached to it:

> There is an opportunity cost for failing to take a decision. A very big cost. Look at the pain we're enduring today with respect to the annual deficit, which was probably avoidable had somebody done something about it a decade ago when it was apparent. And people were concerned then, but action wasn't taken. Now, you know, is that a big scandal? Or is it just bad management. Is it good politics? I don't have the answer to that, but we could have avoided all this and had some other issue to be the news of the day.

We also found little proof that governments consider comparative advantage before committing to subsidizing a business. The theory of comparative advantage hinges on the fact that certain regions are more efficient at and adapted to making specific goods or providing specific services. We saw numerous examples where governments had propped up industries for years, ignoring the law of comparative advantage. One was Sydney Steel in Cape Breton, Nova Scotia. Government-sponsored reports had stated over and over again that the steel mill was too far from markets to be economically viable. Governments repeatedly ignored the advice and continued to subsidize the mill; $2 billion later it finally shut down.

By the end of our journey we all agreed that we had discovered a political system that was wasteful and unaccountable, and the finger of blame pointed in all directions. I was told that it was now up to me to choose one of these directions for my next assignment.

As I considered the possibilities, I was reminded of the interview we conducted with long-time parliamentary observer Sean Moore, who maintained that regardless of who was responsible for the current system, the solutions reside with the citizen. He threw down the gauntlet: "If Canadians want to influence public policy, they really have to take it upon themselves to learn about how our governmental system operates. Unfortunately our educational system is not very good at teaching that."

But it was Alan Ross, a former federal deputy minister of supply and services, who pushed me over the edge:

> If you yourself wanted to go and say, "I want to know, I want to know what the cost of the Indian program is, I want to know what the cost of the Old Age Security Program is, or the young offenders' program, you would have a very difficult time to understand what those costs were, and you would have an even more difficult time trying to find out what anybody was going to do about it. Has anybody asked to see the financial operations of the Department of Health and Welfare or National Defence? So if nobody asked the question, nobody cares! If nobody cares, who cares?

I had my directions. I took up the challenge. I would follow the money to find out how government works.

In 1997 when I started my search for a suitable spending program to investigate, a federal election campaign was on and the Canada Infrastructure Works Program was being talked about by all political parties. The Liberal government had implemented the program as soon as it took office and now, four years later, boasted of its success in creating jobs, proudly crowing that the involvement of provinces and municipalities had fostered harmonious relations among the three levels of government.

The opposition parties fired back that the program had been used to buy votes and the spending had only added to the national debt.

Considering the controversy and the media attention, I decided that the Canada Infrastructure Works Program would be the perfect choice for my project. CIWP had several elements in its favour as a case study. Compared to the decades-old health-care and education programs it was very short term. It was also reasonable to think that I could obtain objective opinions about and analyses of the program's successes and failures since it was unlikely that Canadians would get caught up in emotion about fixing potholes and repairing sewers in the way that they do when it comes to their health services and children's education.

At the outset the government had identified three main goals that CIWP was designed to accomplish: repair core infrastructure, create jobs and improve the economy. I assumed that because these goals were clear, tangible and quantifiable, it would be easy to compare the results of the program against its stated goals and objectives.

Like I said, I made a lot of wrong assumptions in those days.

But before we get into the details of what I and my team of researchers found during our investigations, let's delve a little deeper into the history of the program and how it came to be.

In 1993 the infrastructure program was the centrepiece of the Liberals' election platform and their most expensive campaign promise. They committed $2 billion in federal funding, to be matched by an equal amount from the provincial and municipal governments over two years, to provide a quick boost to an economy with an unemployment rate that seemed stuck above 10 percent. Just three days into the 1993 election campaign, Prime Minister Kim Campbell predicted that there would not be any significant job recovery before 2000, a statement that earned her heckles from angry construction workers in Toronto. In a speech at a Toronto union hall, Opposition leader Jean Chrétien responded to Campbell's comment, saying that if elected, his government would immediately attack the unemployment problem by creating jobs through the infrastructure program.

Chrétien believed the infrastructure program was the key to renewing consumer confidence, which would pull the country out of recession:

It's a program which will create short-term jobs and which will give stimulus to the economy in order to restore confidence in society ... when you go across Canada at the present time and go into the streets and see people, all you see is bankruptcy, unemployment. Nobody wants to spend. But when they see trucks, when they see workers, when they see people moving in cities, then hope is restored at that time. Then you can see this part of the economy recovering.[2]

The Liberals, of course, won the election, and during their first term in power the program was stretched to three years and then to five. However, after being elected into office the Liberals soon recognized the seriousness of continuing to run deficits and adding to the debt. One of their major responses was to reduce the $18 billion in transfer payments paid to the provinces to help fund services like health care and education. The provinces were told that within two years they would have only $11 billion with which to pay for such programs. The premiers complained that the federal government had downloaded its problems onto the provinces. Undoubtedly this growing provincial discontent played an important role in the Liberals' announcement in December 1996 — just months prior to the next federal election — that Ottawa would be entering into negotiations with the provinces to add more money to the $6 billion already invested in the infrastructure program. (Despite these efforts the Liberal majority was reduced by 20 seats in the 1997 election, including 11 losses in Nova Scotia and six defeats in New Brunswick.) The 1997 Throne Speech, which detailed the government's plans for the next four years, signalled a change in policy that included a new era of co-operation. The speech contained 18 references to "partners" and "partnership" as Ottawa pledged to restore harmony with the provinces. The Liberals frequently referred to CIWP as the model for future shared programs.

Here's how the program worked: each level of government — federal, provincial and municipal — was required to pay one-third of the costs of each project undertaken, and each level had input into the program. Municipalities would apply to a provincial or territorial management committee for approval of infrastructure projects, and in some cases the private sector was encouraged to apply in place of municipalities. Management committees were struck in each province and co-chaired by a federal public servant from the regional development agency based in that area. Alongside the federal public servant sat a provincial representative of the ministry involved. It was the role of the management committees to accept project applications from the municipalities, provinces and the private sector, and to sift through the projects and recommend which ones should be funded. The federal government said this method of bottom-up decision making was proof that the three levels of government could work together. The Liberals pointed to the fact that the smooth relations were a welcome contrast to the turmoil and dissension that characterized negotiations between Ottawa and the provinces during the debates over the Meech Lake and Charlottetown accords.

The federal government was also interested in extending its new-found spirit of co-operation beyond the provincial level to the municipalities of the nation. According to the Constitution, responsibility for municipalities falls solely under provincial jurisdiction; yet in the fall of 1997 Ottawa created a 16-member federal caucus to deal with municipal affairs. It was headed by Ontario MP Bryon Wilfert, the former president of the Federation of Canadian Municipalities, and was intended to focus on issues that are common to the federal, provincial and municipal governments.

Ottawa was extremely vocal in its claims that the needs and requests of local governments and communities would be the primary consideration in determining which projects would receive funding under the infrastructure program. Marlene Catterall, parliamentary secretary to the president of the Treasury Board, described the decision-making process in this way:

> In every province projects will be submitted to a joint management committee by municipalities, by school boards and by other local groups. This means that the local level, the communities across Canada, will be the key to the program. The projects that local governments are willing to approve, the projects that local communities identify as their priorities, will be the projects that make up Infrastructure Works.
>
> This is truly rebuilding Canada from the grassroots up, rebuilding Canada in a democratic and equal way across the country.[3]

Indeed, it seemed the federal government couldn't heap enough praise on CIWP: the program would encourage new partnerships and intergovernmental co-operation; it would create jobs for out-of-work Canadians and give a boost to a sagging economy; and it would improve the lives of citizens across the country by addressing the infrastructure needs of their local communities. The reality, however, as we shall see in the chapters to come, was that the program frequently failed to deliver on these promises. From the very beginning it was plagued by problems of mismanagement, careless record keeping, internal squabbling and a basic lack of accountability for decision making — a far cry from the ideal model of cost sharing and intergovernmental co-operation that the Liberals made it out to be.

NOTES

1. Tom McMillan, "The Federal Role in Municipal Water Infrastructure," *Proceedings of First Canadian Conference on Urban Infrastructure* (Edmonton, Alberta: Sodanell Canada Inc., 1987) p. 200. The conference was held in Toronto, Ontario, from February 5–6, 1987.
2. Jean Chrétien, comments made in televised leaders' debate, October 3, 1993.
3. Canada, Parliament, House of Commons, *Debates*, Vol. 133, no. 42 (March 22, 1994) p. 2602.

CHAPTER 2

*67

In 1997 when I began my investigation, the Canada Infrastructure Works Program was in its fourth year, with $6 billion worth of public money having been spent to fund more than 12,000 projects. The legwork began when I contacted the federal department in charge of administering CIWP, the Treasury Board Secretariat in Ottawa. I hoped it could provide me with details on the projects funded by the program. "You are doing what?" Treasury Board staffers asked. "That sounds pretty boring for you." They weren't the last officials not to take my interest seriously.

During the following weeks I made countless phone calls asking for basic information about the application process and the ways in which decisions were made. I either hit voice-mail dead ends or was bounced among officials in Treasury Board and promised that someone would call back. I'm still waiting for some of my calls to be returned.

I soon felt that I was really inconveniencing these people. The public servants just weren't used to answering questions from curious citizens asking how their tax dollars were being spent. Increasing my frustration, the government's communications people kept changing jobs, and with every new contact I made I had to explain, yet again, who I was, what I was doing, and defend my work.

I got so frustrated at the number of times I was forced to leave messages that I began using Bell Canada's *67 feature to block out my name and number so the bureaucrats wouldn't know it was me calling again. To test my theory that they were ignoring me, I'd make a phone call and after I was greeted by voice mail I would hang up. I would call right back and then press *67. I can't tell you how many times the phone was picked up on the first ring. I can still hear them forcing a smile into their voices when they realized it was me.

Whenever I encountered a new contact, I was told that the person I had been dealing with previously was either away on holiday, enrolled in French language training or had been moved to another department. The next thing I would hear was, "Sorry, I'm new to the job." This high rotation of public servants removed the corporate memory of the department, preventing me from getting answers about the way government works. I was, however, getting a very good idea of how the public service works!

Although the Treasury Board of Canada was in charge of administering the infrastructure program, the federal representatives on the management committees were from the respective regional development agencies in each province. As such, my questions about specific project information were often referred to the provincial government ministries involved. In Ontario, for example, there were three ministries that handled different aspects of the program, and in B.C. there were two. The attendance record for the New Brunswick management committee meeting of April 29, 1994, shows that 11 officials from the federal and provincial governments were seated around the table.

Considering the large number of public servants involved in the committees — the decision-making bodies for the program — I expected that CIWP would be administered to a high standard that justified the government's decision to replicate it when creating future cost-sharing programs. It didn't take long for me to become disabused of this notion.

Dredging through piles of newspaper articles from the early days of the program, I came across a 1994 report in *The Globe and Mail* stating that the federal ridings that had elected Liberal MPs had been rewarded with higher amounts of money than ridings that had elected either Reform or Bloc Québécois MPs. The article claimed that 90 of 176 Liberal ridings had received infrastructure funds averaging $5.38 million per riding, while 51 Reform ridings were granted an average of $2.18 million and 53 Bloc ridings averaged $2.7 million. The article pointed out that the information had been obtained through the federal government's Access to Information Act.[1]

This information raised questions about the decision-making processes and criteria used to determine who received infrastructure funding. To find out what had transpired in those years since the article had been written, I called Treasury Board and asked for an updated summary of the total amounts received by each federal *party*. I was told that the federal government had not tracked the projects by *party*: "The data quoted in the news article was extracted from a unique report which has not been updated. No other records exist on this matter."[2]

I subsequently found a copy of a press release published shortly after the article appeared in 1994. The release indicated that it did appear as if a disproportionate amount of money had gone to Liberal ridings, but pointed out that the allegations of favouritism were misleading — the inequities were actually a result of the fact that few projects had been handed out in the predominantly Bloc Québécois ridings in Quebec or the Reform ridings in B.C. The press release also explained that most provinces handed out infrastructure money based on population, meaning that the densely populated urban ridings received more money than the sparsely populated rural ones. Most urban ridings had elected Liberal MPs in the 1993 election (urban voters, in fact, had pushed the Liberal Party to its majority victory), which explained the high number of infrastructure grants to projects in the governing party's ridings.[3]

I conceded that I had been stopped in my tracks. I wasn't prepared to give up, but where to next? *The Globe and Mail* had obtained information using the Access to Information Act. Couldn't I do the same if I had some expert help to guide me through this unfamiliar bureaucratic maze? After a few calls to friends who are journalists, I was put in touch with Mike Dagg, a retired librarian who, I was confidently told, knows exactly how to get information out of the government.

Part of Mike's appeal is that he knows every word of the Access to Information Act and every loophole public servants use to refuse the release of information. His reputation as a tenacious researcher was solidified a few years earlier when, after seven years, he won an Access case that the federal government fought all the way to the Supreme Court of Canada. In the months to come Mike would become my Sherpa!

During our initial, three-hour meeting I told him about my work and the methodology I had used to study the Canada Infrastructure Works Program. His first reaction was to warn me that my problems would be three times tougher than usual because of the different levels of government involved. Then he gave me my first significant lesson in unlocking government secrets. He told me not to rely on government-produced calculations; I should go after raw data, such as project listings that describe each project, along with its cost and location. He said public servants have a tough time justifying a decision to withhold raw data from the public. With the raw data in my hands, I could sort the information on my own and draw my own conclusions. Like a battle-seasoned cynic, he warned me that I would still meet some resistance when requesting raw data because public servants worry that the information will be misinterpreted or interpreted differently than the government would like; a single interpretation by all makes it neat and tidy for the government because it avoids all contradictions to the official spin.

If I wanted an update of what had happened since the 1994 story had appeared, I would have to obtain a master list of all projects and sort them by federal electoral riding to figure out which MPs and parties were the winners of the infrastructure sweepstakes. I called the Treasury Board again and requested a list of projects funded by the Infrastructure Works Program from 1994 to the present. A few days later I received several computer disks containing the master list up to the fall of 1997. The information listed location, applicant, total eligible cost and federal share, and contained a brief description of each project and the total number of jobs created by the project.[4]

There was no way to sort all 12,628 projects in a reasonable time, so I selected two provinces, Alberta and Ontario, to try to determine whether there was any favouritism in the funding distribution across the country. Alberta elected 20 Reform MPs in 1993, while the Liberals had been held to only four seats. In contrast, in Ontario 98 Liberals were elected and only one Reform candidate won a seat.

I armed myself with the Treasury Board's list for Alberta and Ontario, gathered a few good road maps and purchased the Elections Canada booklets that list the riding locations for every city, town and hamlet in the country. I then prepared myself for a month of paper shuffling as I placed each project in its respective federal riding.

I soon realized that I wouldn't be able to complete the job because there wasn't enough specific information to locate each of the projects. For instance, there wasn't enough detail to distinguish between the two Ontario towns called Atwood, or the two called Wallace, or the two Limericks. The problems were not limited to a select few names. When I tried to sort the projects in Toronto, the task became impossible; there are 36 ridings in and around Toronto, yet under the category for "applicant information," data, in some cases, was presented only for "Toronto." In the Ontario database of 5,022 projects, I was unable to place 1,496 of them because there wasn't enough detail attached to the location of school boards, or to another designation called "other unincorporated community." I found the same problems sorting information for Alberta.

Because each project had a unique number assigned to it, I assumed that a public servant with Treasury Board would be able to use this number to call up files that contained more detail. The identification number could then be cross-referenced with the project to provide me with more information so that I could find the appropriate riding.

It wasn't that easy.

When I asked for more detail on a location, Treasury Board officials told me I would have to provide the infrastructure office with a list of the specific identification numbers with which I was having trouble. I would then be supplied a CSD, a census subdivision number, to identify the project. I would have to take that number to the Statistics Canada office to request a copy of their CSD maps. I could then trace the CSD number, locate it on the maps, slot it into its federal riding — et voilà!

Eventually, however, I was forced to abandon the search in Alberta and Ontario — I discovered that Elections Canada had redrawn almost all of the federal electoral ridings between 1993 and 1997, meaning that the infrastructure data for the previous four years would be skewed. The thought of a conspiracy crossed my mind. I had no choice but to move on to another province.

I embarked on a third case study, sorting the projects in the politically volatile province of New Brunswick — volatile because New Brunswickers elected nine Liberals and one Tory in the 1993 election, but flipped in 1997, electing five Tories and two New Democrats and reducing the Liberals to three seats.

Even in this relatively small, 10-riding province, I hit stumbling blocks in my attempts to line up projects with their federal ridings. Out of a total of 351 projects, I couldn't locate 38 of them — more than 10 percent — because several places weren't on my maps from Elections Canada, nor were they on a provincial road map. I called my relatives in Fredericton for help but they hadn't heard of places like Crane Mountain or Bas-Neguac. I called the New Brunswick Ministry of Municipalities, Culture and Housing, the provincial ministry in charge of administering the program. When I was finally connected to someone authorized to speak with me, he said he was stumped by my questions but promised to call me back with the answers. A few days later he phoned and read me the relevant press releases, and together we talked it out until I was able to locate most of the outstanding projects.

Regardless of whom I was speaking with or what government material I was reading, the fact about the program that was always trumpeted was that the money was to be distributed among all 10 federal electoral ridings in New Brunswick. That was how I found out that all ridings in the province were granted an equal amount of $12.2 million in the first phase of the program. But my records stated that there was $150 million in infrastructure money to be handed out in New Brunswick.[5] The numbers didn't add up.

After the sorting was complete my research indicated that the distribution in New Brunswick was anything but equal. I discovered that the riding of Acadie–Bathurst in the northeastern part of the province, with a total population of 87,613, had received more than $26 million for 58 projects up to November 1997. At the other end of the scale was the riding of Tobique–Mactaquac, which is along the U.S. border and has a population of 62,525. As of November 1997, Tobique–Mactaquac had received just over $11 million for 34 projects.[6] I filed a Right to Information request with the province, asking government officials to explain the imbalance.

According to the information I received, the difference came about because the program's decision makers had designated 20

32

percent, or $30.5 million, of the total funds available for "projects strategic to the province, or projects that overlap a number of the regions."[7] There didn't seem to be any hard-and-fast rules on strategic projects, leaving the door open to a wide interpretation of what was important to the province.

It's interesting to note that the riding of Liberal Cabinet minister Doug Young, Acadie–Bathurst, received the most infrastructure money, more than $8 million from Ottawa alone; yet his constituents seemed to buck the conventional wisdom that politicians benefit from spending announcements — they shunned him in 1997 and he was not re-elected. At the same time the riding of Tobique–Mactaquac turned its back on its Liberal MP and elected a Tory. Evidently, in a region with a high percentage of seasonal workers, the photo opportunities and ribbon cuttings for infrastructure projects couldn't overcome the hostility that had resulted from Ottawa's cuts to the Employment Insurance Program.

During a family visit to Fredericton over Christmas I followed up on some outstanding questions that had resulted from my recent survey of New Brunswick. I filed several minor Right to Information requests and told the government officials that I was just visiting to question how long it takes for requests to move through the approval process. I really hoped to find out how a provincial government handled its files and organized its applications for funding.

When I arrived at Marysville Place outside Fredericton, the building that houses the provincial ministry dealing with infrastructure, an assistant met me at the reception desk. She was more co-operative than most of the public servants I had encountered thus far in my investigation, inviting me into the office where the records were kept. I can't help but suspect her willingness to assist me had a lot to do with the fact that the office was virtually empty because of the holidays — in other words, she didn't have to worry about anyone looking over her shoulder or being chastised by an overly suspicious superior for showing documents to an "outsider." She gave me some information on the program and even opened a couple of files on projects that had yet to be accepted. I was surprised to see several flimsy, handwritten applications for tens of thousands of dollars that were incomplete because the estimates of jobs created by the project had not been filled in.

The omission of the number of jobs to be created flew right in the face of the government's essential project criteria. The government stated that the promise of job creation was vital to the appeal of a project: "While criteria are not weighted, short- and long-term job creation as well as the longer-term economic and environmental benefits are important objectives of the program."[8]

There was also an application for $80,000 to construct a building at the Moncton airport for the large American courier company FedEx. A little voice inside my head asked, "Why does a successful American courier company need a subsidy to erect a building at the Moncton airport?"

As I was leaving I explained to the assistant that I was looking to find out what criteria were used when choosing projects and distributing money throughout the province. She leaned over to me, like a conspirator, cupped her hand over the side of her mouth and whispered, "Oh, it's all political."

Truer words were never spoken. My apprenticeship was over.

When I got back to Ottawa I called the Treasury Board asking for a sample of the Infrastructure Works application form. I was bothered by the applications I had seen in Fredericton. There must be a standard form used for applications, I thought, to make it easier to judge and handle each project. Yet the forms I had seen had been anything but standard. I was told that there were no hard-and-fast rules forced on this program by the federal government. Some applicants chose to use standard forms; some didn't and created their own.

By this time officials with Treasury Board must have sensed my frustration. They offered me a face-to-face meeting with the public servants in charge of the program. Mike Dagg attended the meeting with me — I asked him to come along to serve as an extra set of ears in case the bureaucrats tried to baffle me with obscure references to the Access to Information Act. On the other side of the table sat Randy Poon, Treasury Board's senior analyst for the infrastructure program, along with Brian Biggar, Treasury Board communications advisor, and Monique Leblanc-McCulloch, a senior analyst with the Office of the Information Commissioner assigned to the Treasury Board.

The highlight of the meeting came when I asked for clarification on one Ontario project. Randy Poon reached over to a set of large blue binders stacked at the end of the boardroom table to find the answer. That was when he revealed the Holy Grail of the infrastructure program:

a list of projects broken down by *riding*. The information had been sorted in such a way that all he had to do was group the ridings by party and add up the total dollars spent to calculate the amount of money that went to each party.

I asked myself, "How in the hell had they been able to get around my Access request for a breakdown of projects by party?" I reminded Randy that the government had told me that no such list existed. He said he recalled handling my request but, he pointed out, my request was for a breakdown by *party* — not by *riding*!

I gave myself a mental slap on the wrist for being too loose with my descriptions in my Access request. In the future I would carefully consider my words when posing questions to the public service. When Monique handed back my original request she said, "We aren't trying to hide anything." I didn't respond. Lesson learned.

I asked for the blue binders and was told that I could have a copy if I paid $165 to cover the photocopying charges and the manual labour to make the copies. I paid. When I received my very own copy of this infrastructure bible — worth a lot more to me than $165 — I found an error that provided me with a concrete example of how accountability can be blurred in a cost-sharing program. Sorting through the Ontario list of projects, I noticed that the Seagram Stadium had received infrastructure money. According to the federal government's database, the stadium, located in Kitchener–Waterloo, had been attributed to the riding of London–Middlesex, a one-hour drive to the west.[9]

I called Treasury Board to notify it of the mistake and to ask how it could have occurred. My contact blamed the bookkeeping error on his provincial counterparts. He told me that there were some problems with the flow of information and that sometimes he only received project information on paper — not electronically. Moreover, some of the project descriptions were very vague, leaving it up to him to classify the projects and chase down details. This new information shook my confidence in the accuracy of the blue binders. No one level of government seemed to have a firm grip on the administration of the program.

Closer examination of the information in the blue binders failed to give me the breakdown of total infrastructure dollars per party. One stumbling block was that the projects had been classified and sorted based on the benefit to a "single" riding or to "multiple" ridings. A project that would provide a benefit to a single riding was obvious, but all projects less than $750,000 were automatically considered single-riding benefit projects, regardless of how many ridings were involved. For example, a $500,000 project to repair a sewer line would be classified as "single riding," even if the sewer stretched across two ridings.

There were several problems with the projects listed under "multiple riding benefits." To begin with, it was not always clear which riding benefited from the spending. For example, the federal government contributed $9.2 million to a project to rehabilitate schools located within the jurisdiction of the Toronto Board of Education (total cost of the project was $27 million). As I looked over the records, I noticed that the benefits, for 116 schools, were all credited to only one riding (Don Valley West). In other cases several ridings were each attributed the *full cost* of a project. The $57-million project to construct a deep storage tunnel along the Lake Ontario shoreline, for example, was listed as a multiple-riding benefit, but the blue books attributed the full cost of the project to *each* of the three ridings involved (Parkdale–High Park, Rosedale and Trinity–Spadina). Moreover, each riding was also given full credit for the creation of 855 short-term jobs.

Keeping in mind all the problems with the lists, the three ridings that received the most federal money under the category of "single-riding benefits" were

- the Reform riding of Okanagan–Similkameem–Merrit (B.C.) with 29 projects costing Ottawa $17 million;
- the Liberal riding of Waterloo (Ontario) with 44 projects costing the federal government $9.6 million; and
- the Liberal riding of Simcoe North (Ontario) with 80 projects costing the federal government $9.4 million.

The ridings that received the most federal money under the category of "multiple-riding benefits" were

- the Liberal riding of Trinity–Spadina (Ontario) with 24 projects costing the federal government $86 million;
- the Reform riding of Delta (B.C.) with one project that cost Ottawa $68 million; and
- the BQ riding of Québec (Quebec) with three projects costing Ottawa $31 million.[10]

As I pored over the information outlined in the blue books, I was disappointed to find that their only real benefit was that they showed which types of projects were delivered in each riding. But what really started to get my attention were the projects that didn't exactly fit my definition of "infrastructure" — the "new municipal golf clubhouse facility" in the riding of St. John's East, for example, and the upgrades to the CFL's Hamilton Tiger Cats' football stadium. What happened to roads, sewers and bridges?

It was time for me to find out more about how this whole infrastructure program idea was conceived.

NOTES

1. Canadian Press, "Infrastructure money flows to repairs in Liberal riding," *The Globe and Mail*, November 4, 1994, p. A9.
2. Michael Calcott, Co-ordinator, Access to Information and Privacy, Ministerial and Executive Services, Treasury Board Secretariat, [letter], October 17, 1997. Response to Access to Information request filed by Jay Innes on September 22, 1997.
3. *Story on Infrastructure Funding Favouritism Misleading* [media release], Office of the Minister Responsible for Infrastructure, November 4, 1994.
4. Infrastructure Works Office, Treasury Board Secretariat, Canada Infrastructure Works Project List [worksheet on computer disk]. Master list of 12,628 Canada Infrastructure Works Projects from 1994 to October 31, 1997.
5. *Canada Infrastructure Works: Federal-Provincial Partnerships* [media release], Government of Canada, Canada Infrastructure Works, Ottawa, February 18, 1994.
6. Infrastructure Works Office, Treasury Board Secretariat, Canada Infrastructure Works Project List [worksheet on computer disk]. Master list of 12,628 Canada Infrastructure Works Projects from 1994 to October 31, 1997.
7. Ann Breault, Minister, Department of Municipalities, Culture and Housing, Canada/New Brunswick Infrastructure Program [letter],

January 14, 1998. Response to Right to Information request filed by Jay Innes.

8. *Canada Infrastructure Works: Federal-Provincial Partnerships* [media release], Government of Canada, Canada Infrastructure Works, Ottawa, February 18, 1994.

9. Infrastructure Works Office, Treasury Board Secretariat, Canada Infrastructure Works, Project Listing by Riding (Blue Books). List of all infrastructure projects approved as of March 4, 1997.

10. Infrastructure Works Office, Treasury Board Secretariat, Canada Infrastructure Works, Project Listing by Riding (Blue Books). List of all infrastructure projects approved as of March 4, 1997.

CHAPTER 3

The Big Fix

The first call for a national infrastructure program funded by the federal government came in the mid-1980s from the Federation of Canadian Mayors and Municipalities (FCMM), the predecessor of the Federation of Canadian Municipalities (FCM). According to the FCMM, the country was in need of $15 billion of infrastructure repair. The report warned that if something wasn't done to combat the decline in sewer and water conditions, raw sewage from our cities and towns would continue to pollute our waterways. The report also stated that the decline in the condition of roads and bridges threatened to harm our economy because potential investors and tourists would not be attracted to Canada.

When we interviewed Harry Gaudet, chief administrative officer for the City of Charlottetown, he said the FCM adopted the position that the municipalities shouldn't be the only ones paying for the maintenance of the country's infrastructure:

> The provincial and federal governments are collecting gasoline tax, excise tax, corporate and sales tax, and some of those

taxes could justifiably be diverted into the maintenance of our road and street systems as well as the maintenance and upgrading of our bridges, sidewalks, storm sewer systems and our water systems. And the FCM members feel that a portion of those taxes should be reinvested in the maintenance of our municipal infrastructure.

But the Mulroney government did not support the federation's proposal. Environment Minister Tom McMillan was given the job of reminding the municipalities that, under the Constitution, their affairs were the responsibility of the provinces. He then told them that Ottawa was doing its part to maintain the country's infrastructure by dealing with, among other things, the pollution problems in the Halifax and Hamilton harbours.

In July 1987 Minister McMillan faced the wrath of the country's municipal leaders at the First Canadian Conference on Urban Infrastructure. While he did recognize that there was an infrastructure problem, acknowledging that eight million Canadians live in municipalities that do not treat their sewage, he suggested that municipal leaders adopt a user-fee system of billing to address their problems. Having people pay for the water they consume, he said, would have a direct impact on the behaviour of Canadians because they would conserve water to save money. And the policy would increase revenues that could be used to pay for infrastructure repairs since those who used a high volume of water would have to pay more. The idea was generally frowned upon because Canadians consider water to be a free good that should be accessible to everyone, in the same way health and education programs are universally available.

The Liberal Party, sitting in Opposition under John Turner, endorsed the FCM's "Big Fix," a $15-billion plan to upgrade the nation's aging roads, bridges, sewers and water lines, and made it an integral part of its 1988 election strategy.[1] The Liberals promised to spend $5 billion to upgrade municipal facilities. They pointed out that the nation's roads, sewers, bridges, storm sewers and water treatment plants were 20 years old on average and that the federal government was avoiding its obligation to repair and update them. "There are some things we all take for granted," stated Turner in the run-up to the election, "clean water, fresh air, safe bridges, good roads, an efficient sewage system, that is, until they breakdown.... These basic requirements for everyday life are slowly eroding because of the cynical neglect of the Mulroney government."[2]

The election debate focused on the pros and cons of entering into a free trade agreement with the United States. The Liberals, who opposed the agreement, promised that the infrastructure program would create 314,000 jobs, a number that exceeded the estimates attached to free trade.[3] Of course, the Conservatives won the 1988 election and the Liberals were denied the opportunity to prove these claims.

In 1991, members of the private sector jumped onboard, publicly supporting the infrastructure program at the Transportation Association of Canada's annual convention in Winnipeg. Here, the Coalition to Renew Canada's Infrastructure announced its creation and joined forces with the Federation of Canadian Municipalities and the Canadian Construction Association. The coalition was headed by John Redfern, chairman of the national construction company Lafarge Corporation, and was made up of 20 Canadian corporations representing a variety of businesses, from the manufacturing sector to suppliers and contractors. The coalition justified the need for an infrastructure program by quoting a study from 1988–1989 that claimed that the money needed for essential road maintenance surpassed what was being spent by nearly $3 billion.[4]

In the House of Commons, the Liberal Opposition continued to push for a national infrastructure program. On March 25, 1992, the Liberal MP for Ottawa–Vanier, Jean-Robert Gauthier, stood up in the House and described a number of the infrastructure horror stories that were plaguing Canada. He noted that "every day 500,000 litres of wastewater are dumped into the St. Lawrence," and in Newfoundland "more than 48,000 homes do not have adequate water and sewage services, and 80 percent of the population drinks improperly treated water."[5] The Liberals continued to make the case that federal involvement in municipal affairs was not an intrusion into an area that is provincial jurisdiction; they justified taking action because the infrastructure problem was really a problem of *pollution*, which is a federal responsibility.

At the same time the FCM, which first realized the seriousness of the infrastructure decline in the country, was willing to amend its proposal for federal funding plans to include contributions from all three levels of government and the private sector. When our research team spoke with Ron Hayter, past president of the FCM, he said the federation had to stretch its definition of infrastructure to get all parties to accept the program:

> The program we put together was a three-pronged approach. We would concentrate on the importance of repairing the crumbling infrastructure in Canada. That was absolutely essential. Secondly, we were in the midst of an economic downturn in Canada, so we wanted to emphasize the importance of doing this work to create jobs at a time when a lot of people were out of work. And thirdly, we wanted to emphasize the fact that good infrastructure in your community was important from the standpoint of attracting industry and business to your community. It was a part of making Canada more competitive. That was the approach. It was a lot more sexy than the earlier approach that we used in 1986, where we were only concentrating on traditional, basic infrastructure.

When Jean Chrétien replaced John Turner as leader of the Opposition, he continued his party's support of the infrastructure program. In a letter to *The Vancouver Sun* in June 1992, Chrétien stated, "Their [our cities'] physical infrastructure is falling apart."[6] The endorsement of a cost-sharing infrastructure program earned the support of the Laborers' International Union during the 1993 election, when it presented Chrétien with a gold shovel in a widely publicized photo opportunity.

Then, in a politically adept move, the Chrétien Liberals told Canadians that, if elected, they would rip up the Tories' $4.8-billion contract to purchase 15 anti-submarine helicopters and use the money to pay for the infrastructure program. This statement gave the public the impression that the infrastructure program would be a painless investment because it had, in effect, already been paid for — so taxpayers wouldn't have to fork over any new money. The political spin avoided the fact that the federal and provincial governments were mired in deficit and debt and the money used to pay for such large investments — whether on helicopters or infrastructure — would have to be borrowed and paid back with interest in the following years.[7]

The Canada Infrastructure Works Program was the most expensive election promise outlined in the Liberals' 1993 *Red Book*, which committed the federal government to pay $2 billion of the $6-billion cost-shared program. By this time the definition of infrastructure had expanded beyond the traditional sewage and water projects called for a year earlier by MP Gauthier in the House of Commons. According to *The Red Book*, infrastructure included "undertakings for the common benefit, such as transportation and communications links and water and sewage systems." The objective of all the work was to make Canada more competitive while fixing pollution problems that would help the environment and improve the overall health of the country. The advances in mass transit and telecommunications would increase the country's expertise in these areas and create new products that could be exported, boosting our national economy. Finally, the Liberals promised to create "immediate high-paying direct and indirect jobs for Canadians, particularly in the construction and manufacturing sectors."[8]

After the election these goals were reiterated by Art Eggleton, the new president of the Treasury Board and the minister responsible for infrastructure, in his maiden speech in the House of Commons:

> Throughout the industrialized world, the last few years have seen a very active, renewed interest in the role and the importance of infrastructure, whether it is for economic competitiveness to attract investment, environmental protection and improvement, the quality of public amenities or the quality of life in general. For these reasons, and despite extremely difficult fiscal constraints which we are well aware of, the Liberal Party chose to undertake a major co-operative program of infrastructure renewal as one of the central planks of its election platform.[9]

During debate in the House of Commons, the Liberal government said the program would reduce the infrastructure repair costs that would have to be paid by future generations. It promised the money spent on the program would quickly inject cash into the economy and create more than 100,000 jobs.

The Opposition didn't buy it. It struck back saying that the government funds spent on frivolous projects would only increase the national debt, which would eventually have to be tackled by future generations. The Bloc Québécois and the Reform Party also rejected the program because they felt it was a federal intrusion into provincial affairs. As projects were approved and word circulated that the program was not being confined to repairing roads, sewers, water mains and bridges, Ontario Reform MP Ed Harper questioned whether the costs and benefits had been considered before making the spending decisions:

> With respect to each of the following projects, what was the result of the cost-benefit analysis conducted by the office of the minister responsible for infrastructure: (a) the construction of a park building and a canoe hall of fame in Shawinigan, Quebec;[10] (b) the construction of bocce courts in Toronto, Ontario; (c) renovations to Northlands Coliseum and Ducey Park reconstruction in Edmonton, Alberta; (d) renovations to the Calgary Saddledome in Calgary, Alberta; (e) removal of overhead wires in Shelburne, Nova Scotia; (f) construction of a world-class marina at Lewisporte Harbour by Gateway Development Inc. in Newfoundland; (g) development of two residential development areas for the Ebb and Flow First Nation; (h) redeveloping duck pond gardens in Winnipeg, Manitoba; (i) air-conditioning a community hall in the village of Debden, Saskatchewan; and (j) construction of a building to accommodate circus training and production facilities for Cirque du Soleil in Montreal, Quebec?

Eggleton responded:

> The federal office of infrastructure does not conduct formal cost-benefit analyses of infrastructure project proposals. It is responsible for setting up national framework agreements and reviewing project proposals received from federal implementing agencies and departments.
>
> Costs and benefits are determined at the provincial and local levels. To be eligible for funding under the program, projects submitted by local partners must meet certain provisions of the national criteria established in the framework

agreements between the federal government and the province or territory.[11]

So before the government would grant funding to a particular project, it would have to meet the criteria of a "framework agreement." What Eggleton failed to explain, however, was exactly what these framework agreements were, and what they looked like.

NOTES

1. For a detailed description of the Big Fix plan, see Lois Legge, "Turner backs the 'Big Fix,'" *The Halifax Chronicle-Herald*, June 1, 1987, pp. 1, 16.
2. Joan Bryden, "Turner unveils own election tab," *Calgary Herald*, September 23, 1988, p. A7.
3. Tim Harper, "Turner offers cities $5-billion tune-up," *The Toronto Star*, September 23, 1988, pp. A1–A2.
4. Bud Robertson, "New group bids to stop road decay: government funds drive urged," *Winnipeg Free Press*, September 18, 1991, p. 19.
5. Canada, Parliament, House of Commons, *Debates*, Vol. 7, no. 20 (March 25, 1992) p. 8815.
6. Jean Chrétien (Editorial), "Cities' problems can be solved: Not only can the federal government do something to improve the quality of life in Canada's cities — it must," *The Vancouver Sun*, June 13, 1992, p. A15.
7. In the House on February 23, 1994, David Collenette, then minister of national defence and veterans affairs, stated, "In the last election campaign the Liberal Party promised to cut defence spending by $1.6 billion over four years beginning April 1 of this year. Much of that money that we cut yesterday in the budget will have gone to the national infrastructure program." House of Commons, *Debates*, Vol. 133, no. 28 (February 23, 1994) p. 1743.
8. *Creating Opportunity: The Liberal Plan for Canada (The Red Book)*, (Ottawa: The Liberal Party of Canada, September 1993) pp. 60–61. The referenced pages of the 1993 *Red Book* describe a

Liberal government commitment to undertake infrastructure projects focused on the "common benefit" that would, in turn, meet several objectives:

- By investing in transportation and communication systems the program would have a long-term impact on the nation's economy by improving the movement of supplies and goods more efficiently and at less cost.
- Water and sewage improvements would benefit the environment and the health of the nation that would "result in substantial long-term savings" in both areas.
- The platform also promised to invest in "state-of-the-art infrastructure" to increase the country's expertise in these areas and expand the possible markets for products.
- Infrastructure funding to the areas of mass transit, telecommunications and pollution control would expand the country's international trade.
- Along with all these "long-term benefits" the platform promised to "create immediate high-paying direct and indirect jobs for Canadians," especially in the areas of construction and manufacturing.

9. House of Commons, *Debates*, Vol. 133, no. 5 (January 21, 1994) pp. 137–138.
10. The proposal to build a canoe hall of fame in the prime minister's riding provides a good example of the type of confusion and distortion that surrounded many of the infrastructure projects. Everyone was under the assumption that the hall of fame had been completed, but the project lists that I obtained from the Treasury Board Secretariat indicated that the project had never been approved. I spoke with people involved in the program in Quebec who confirmed that, indeed, the canoe hall of fame had not been approved — and therefore was never built. An official with the Canadian Canoe Museum told me that he had travelled to Shawinigan to discuss the merits of the project, but the proposal seemed to fade away when it began to draw criticism from the media and the public. I made calls to officials with the PMO, asking them to explain why the prime minister had not set the record

straight and informed the media and the public that the canoe hall of fame had not gone ahead. They said they didn't know.

11. House of Commons, *Debates*, Vol. 133, no. 131 (November 25, 1994) p. 8300.

CHAPTER 4

The Rules of the Game

I decided to take a closer look at the nature of the infrastructure agreements struck between the different levels of government.

Reading the MP Info Kit, which was prepared by Canada Infrastructure Works and outlines the details of the program, I discovered that for the purposes of Infrastructure Works, the First Nations had been given $29 million;[1] I therefore assumed that the First Nations had been granted the same status as the provincial and territorial governments. This wasn't long after the TV news reports came out of Davis Inlet in Labrador, showing homes that did not have running water and kids sniffing gas. Government help for infrastructure and job creation in such communities was indeed long overdue.

Nevertheless, the fact that the First Nations were considered an independent level of government under the program raised questions about program administration. Who represented the First Nations in negotiations with the federal government? Who provided the other two-thirds of funding for these projects? Who sat on the management committees along with the federal government representatives?

A call to Treasury Board for answers was passed on to the federal Department of Indian and Northern Affairs. The reaction I received when I phoned its communications branch was similar to the response I received from Treasury Board: "Who are you and what are you doing?" My calls once again bounced around the government halls; the most helpful response I received was a suggestion to check the department's Web site for answers. As I clicked through the site's pages and links, I wondered where all the simple answers were buried.

In an attempt to show that I was really interested in understanding the First Nations component of the program, I called the communications department back and asked what I thought was an easy question. Could I obtain a copy of the Canada–First Nations Infrastructure Works Program agreement? There was a long pause, followed by a weary sigh, and then I was told that there was no agreement.

The communications person informed me that the minister of Indian and northern affairs made the spending decisions. There were no management committees to sort through and select projects. I asked how a program is administered when there aren't any hard-and-fast rules. Another sigh before she told me the program was administered in the same way all programs are administered through the department. When I told her I had no idea how programs are administered through the department, she said in a voice that reminded me of my high school English teacher — who had the ability to slip in a threat while lecturing me — "You'd better find out." To dismiss my suspicion about the lack of accountability in the program, she ended the call by assuring me that the program complied with environmental regulations and that the department reports to the auditor general.

Despite this claim, in 1996 the auditor general of Canada did not report on the First Nations' participation in the program. I still haven't been able to find out whether the federal government did in fact foot the whole bill, or if there were other levels of government or parties sharing the cost of the projects on First Nations' reserves.

But Treasury Board eventually did supply me with copies of all the federal-provincial and federal-territorial agreements for the program.

In the case of the Canada–Quebec contract there were two clauses missing that were present in all the other federal-provincial agreements. The Quebec contract did not contain the section that stated that the federal court would adjudicate any disputes between the two levels of government. Why was Quebec exempt? Shouldn't there be a mechanism for settling disputes included in *all* agreements related to spending millions of dollars? The second clause that was missing referred to the Financial Administration Act, legislation that outlines the rules for handling public funds and dates back to the earliest days of Confederation. The FAA is the basis for *all* regulations that govern federal spending.

I went back to my files and found the minutes from the March 1994 meeting of the Standing Committee on Government Operations, which I had accessed over the Internet. Art Eggleton appeared before the committee and opened by explaining that the Treasury Board gets its legislative authority from three federal documents: the Financial Administration Act, the Official Languages Act and the Public Service Staff Relations Act. I took from his comments that the Financial Administration Act must be important; and yet the federal government negotiators had chosen to leave it out of one federal-provincial agreement.

I needed someone who could predict the possible implications of the FAA not being included in an agreement between two governments. I phoned the Library of Parliament and was put in touch with the clerk of the Senate finance committee. He grilled me with all the standard questions, but by this time I had my introduction as well rehearsed as a veteran telemarketer. The clerk coolly told me that he didn't normally provide information to journalists, and in a tone laced with sarcasm he said he would make a couple of calls and then either get back to me — or not! Apparently he chose the second option because that was the last I heard from the clerk of the Senate finance committee.

In my next attempt to find out why the two clauses had been excluded, I called the Treasury Board Secretariat. A person with the media relations department referred me to the Federal Office of Regional Development–Quebec (FORD-Q). I called the FORD-Q headquarters in Montreal and was greeted in French. I responded with "Hello there," thinking the voice on the other end would pick up on the fact that I couldn't speak French and switch to English. He didn't. So I did my best to follow along, but continued to speak in English while he stuck with French. When I requested that my call be returned, the voice on the other end responded with a well-placed "Parfait!"

Within a week another official from FORD-Q contacted me and suggested that the omission of any references to the federal court or to the Financial Administration Act was not unique to the Quebec CIWP agreement, that the Prince Edward Island agreement had similar omissions. I saw a chance to make an impression and show that I had done my homework. I wasn't about to be misled, so I pointed out that she was definitely mistaken; I had a copy of all the agreements and only Quebec's was missing those clauses. Sounding a bit panicked, the FORD-Q official then quickly suggested I phone Richard Lestage, a lawyer for the federal government who worked at the Treasury Board.

I phoned and e-mailed Mr. Lestage with requests to get in touch a number of times before I finally received an e-mail response from a member of the Treasury Board's infrastructure communications team. After two months I was right back were I had started. The media relations person told me that although the FAA wasn't mentioned in the Quebec agreement, it still applied because federal law is supreme. It was the same with the clause about the federal court, which would adjudicate any disputes, regardless of the omission.

But if disputes were going to be adjudicated, why not simply write that clause into the agreement or omit the two references from all agreements? With that logic, why wouldn't the government adopt the same strategy used with the First Nations and not bother writing agreements at all? I pressed for a written copy of the Treasury Board response.

A week or so later another media relations person called to say that she was now handling my file because my previous contact was no longer with the Treasury Board Secretariat. This new officer said that she had the Treasury Board's official response to my question about the missing clauses. But there was a problem. She could not fax me the response because to do so would violate department policy.

I insisted that she double-check. Why would a federal policy prevent bureaucrats from sharing this type of information with a member of the public? When she called me again, a week later, it was with a mixed result. She said the best she could do was to read the Treasury Board's response to me over the phone! I grabbed a pen and she dictated: "Inclusion or exclusion of an otherwise applicable statutory provision does not invalidate nor confer greater validity to the contract. The law remains supreme over any provision found in the contract."

I politely requested to speak with someone who could provide this federal interpretation in writing. She suggested that I contact Treasury

Board legal counsel, Richard Lestage. Him again! I wondered if I could perhaps cut through some of the bureaucratic red tape by mentioning her name when trying to get the elusive Mr. Lestage's attention? She was reluctant to let me use her name, and my attempts at reaching Lestage were met with the same silence as before.

So I filed an Access to Information request for all government documents related to the omission of those two clauses. A one-page response arrived three months later, indicating that there were actually 70 pages of relevant material, but because of exemptions, I wasn't permitted to see any of them.

Not a single line.

Exemptions are permitted under the Access law for a number of reasons. In my case the most common reasons the government used to defend its decision to legally withhold information were that:

- the information could be injurious to federal-provincial relations;
- the material was protected by solicitor-client privilege;
- the records could harm the economic interests of the government; or
- the information might violate the privacy rights of an individual.

Mike Dagg, my Access to Information mentor, suggested I raise the ante on my search by filing an additional request asking for "copies of all documentation, reports and memos created by staff relating to my two questions." What we hoped to get was a paper fingerprint, a document that tracked all my previous Access requests, including any correspondence, e-mails and phone calls, and any other information exchanged among the public servants handling my requests. With such documents I could follow the paper trail and learn the names of the public servants who had dealt with my inquiries. I wanted to know which government officials had an interest in my request.

Weeks later the documents arrived. Included were dates and times when my questions had been dealt with, as well as copies of the e-mails and summaries of communications between public servants. There on paper was the proof that Mr. Lestage had chosen to ignore my phone calls and e-mails; either that or he wasn't permitted to interact with the public. His name was on the sign-off sheets for the seven public servants who had handled my request. I could see from the documents that Lestage had forwarded my original e-mail to another official for advice. Lestage noted his concern that answering my request "raise[d] a political issue."[2] The remaining half-page of the Lestage e-mail was censored under Access law exemptions. I was informed that the e-mail might be injurious to federal-provincial relations if it were made public, and that it contained personal information and was protected by lawyer-client privilege.

Another official had indicated to Lestage that someone named Carole should deal with my request. His reply included this curious comment: "My view is that we should always tell the truth."[3] I was glad to know that a public servant thought the Treasury Board should tell the truth!

The tracking documents showed that my original request had gone all the way to the Privy Council Office (PCO), a powerful advisory body to Cabinet and the prime minister. Knowing that I had caught the attention of the upper reaches of the government gave me some satisfaction. The Privy Council Office employs about 500 people and operates as the prime minister's administrative agency. I would later learn that the PCO handles anything to do with federal-provincial relations, which explained its interest in my questions about the relationship between the governments of Canada and Quebec.[4]

Jean Lapierre, the press secretary to the president of the Treasury Board, had signed off on my Access to Information request. I wondered how a member of the minister's political staff, not a bureaucrat, could get to see a request I made to the public service about the administration of the infrastructure program. I posed this question to the Office of the Information Commissioner of Canada. The answer I received was that the press secretary is part of the minister's politically exempt staff. Although the politically exempt staff members do not play any official role in deciding what information is released to the public, I was told, it is "not unusual" for them to be informed of an Access request.[5] It seems reasonable to assume that the inclusion of politically exempt staff in the flow of Access information is intended to give the minister's staff advance warning of any coming political problems and fallout that might result from an Access to Information request.

In the meantime I had written to the auditor general, whose office was responsible for auditing the infrastructure program. I asked why the

Quebec agreement was different and why the omissions were permitted. The auditor general's response was that he did not look at the rules of the infrastructure program as part of the auditing process. It struck me that to audit a spending program without referring to the rules that governed it was like refereeing a hockey game without knowing the difference between a clean check and a dirty hook. In his letter he said, "It would be more appropriate to raise any questions you have in this area directly with the federal implementing department involved."[6]

Following this advice, I wrote a letter to Marcel Massé, who had recently been named the new president of the Treasury Board and minister responsible for infrastructure. In only 12 days Richard Fadden, assistant secretary of the Treasury Board, responded on behalf of Minister Massé: on the differences between the Quebec agreement and the agreements struck with other provinces and territories, the official position was that each agreement was "unique" and that the program was "tailored to be flexible and responsive to local needs and provincial/territorial priorities." Nowhere in the body of the letter did Fadden acknowledge that Quebec was the only province without the FAA clause. All he stated was, "I assure you that the Canadian government is managing its financial obligations diligently under the CIWP."

One paragraph in Fadden's letter seemed to indicate that there was a simple but unspoken answer to my question: "You undoubtedly know that, under the Access to Information Act, federal institutions process existing documents only and have no obligation to create new documents that may provide a more direct answer to the questions asked."[7]

So far all my questions about the omissions in the Canada–Quebec agreement had been directed at the federal level. Perhaps if I approached Quebec government officials involved with program I might get that "more direct answer."

In Montreal we asked Jacques Chagnon, a Liberal MNA and Quebec's minister of education during the first year of CIWP, if he could explain why the two clauses were removed from the Canada–Quebec agreement. He replied:

The finalization of the agreements between Ottawa, Quebec and the municipalities was done so that Quebec was solely responsible for choosing the files that it would agree to.

We decided to keep this control because we wanted to avoid being caught in projects where the federal government would invest in the creation of an agency which then required an operational budget. Then as soon as the agency was in place, Ottawa would go home, saying, "We did our part." They would set up a centre for anything — an old age home, for instance, which was always a good idea. But afterward they would leave the Quebec government to finance the daily operation of the institutions.

We didn't want to be caught in this again. So we kept control over the choice of projects, with the final approval from the federal government. They weren't thrown out. They still kept a veto right over Quebec's projects. Don't forget that this federal project made a lot of sense since it arrived at a point when unemployment was high in Canada, and particularly so in Quebec.[8]

Later we met Claude Ryan at his Montreal apartment to talk about his tenure as provincial minister in the year before the Parti Québécois defeated the provincial Liberals. Ryan admitted that he was a vocal supporter of the infrastructure program: "I asserted my views in a federal election, something I had not done since I was in Quebec politics. But in 1993 I gave my support to the federal Liberals because of this infrastructure program."

Ryan said he instructed his negotiators not to give Ottawa the upper hand in the program. What I didn't expect to hear was a warning about the powers and influence of the public servants who administered the program:

I had stated at the outset that if I were to be in charge, I did not want to see any kind of interference on the part of our federal friends. I wanted things to be clear. They would be fully informed; we would be fundamentally accountable ... acting in conformity with the roles of the program and the rules upon which we have agreed. But we have to function, and I think they realized it's far better when you function that way than if you leave too much room for interference on the part of federal civil servants.

Don't forget the ministers live above the heads of the people in Ottawa. They evolve in a way that they are the public interpreters of the briefs that they receive from their civil servants. They don't have the flexibility and direct kind of action that we have in Quebec and that speaks in favour of more responsibilities being taken in charge by Quebec and the other provinces as well. I noticed that time and again: the federal ministers in general are not aware of problems in as detailed a way as a minister can be in Quebec.[9]

I felt that at the core of every response I received from everyone I approached was this message: mind your own business and maintain a blind faith that the rules of accountability are intact. But nothing I had heard so far could diminish my growing conviction that the infrastructure program was ignoring federal law and the Constitution by unevenly granting exemptions to federal acts in certain provincial agreements.

It wasn't just the Financial Administration Act omission and the exclusion of any reference to the federal court settling disputes in Quebec that troubled me. The Official Languages Act had been omitted from a few agreements as well. This federal act is considered a cornerstone of Canadian values and in many ways is the most powerful law in Ottawa. Each federal department has an official languages branch that enforces this legislation and the official languages commissioner is an officer of Parliament, in the same way the auditor general is an officer of Parliament.

In all but three of the infrastructure agreements between the Government of Canada and the provinces or territories, the contracts stipulated that public information must be provided in both English and French. Neither the British Columbia nor the Alberta agreement stated that information had to be provided in French; there was no requirement in the Quebec agreement that information be provided in English. Since the program was implemented by the federal government with the provinces acting as Ottawa's agents, shouldn't they *all* have been subject to the Official Languages Act? Considering that the Treasury Board gets its legislative powers from the Financial Administration Act, the Public Service Staff Relations Act and the Official Languages Act, it seemed to me that the federal government had ignored its own rules and regulations when it negotiated the federal-provincial agreements.

I spoke with an investigator for the Office of the Official Languages Commissioner about my discoveries. He joked that I should be working for the commission because I was doing its job, combing through the details of federal agreements for errors and omissions. I was less cavalier about the situation, filing an official complaint about the omissions I had uncovered with the commissioner.

The commission investigated my complaint and came to this conclusion:

> According to the agreement with each province, there is no requirement to provide public information in both official languages and each province is responsible for administering the program in accordance with the agreement and its administrative procedures and guidelines. We also noted that most public information material on the program is distributed to the media by the provinces and that is available in both official languages.
>
> Although the provinces are responsible for the information about the projects in question, we pointed out that the federal departments representing the Treasury Board in the provinces contribute substantially to projects through the infrastructure program. Consequently the federal government, by virtue of its spending power, could negotiate compliance with certain linguistic obligations. With respect to the CIWP, in our view the government, by failing to include language clauses in the federal-provincial agreements, missed an opportunity to influence federal institutions and other levels of government to enhance the vitality of the official language minority communities and support their development.[10]

In the end the commissioner wrote a letter to the president of the Treasury Board recommending that any new federal-provincial agreements negotiated under programs of "national scope" include language clauses. The Treasury Board agreed to implement the recommendations.

When I first started asking questions about the Official Languages Act, it was not my intention to force the government to comply with its own legislation. I wanted to find out where the ultimate responsibility for this program resided. With the ruling from the commissioner of official languages, I had an official source confirm that the federal government was primarily responsible. My discoveries also suggested that federal negotiators had chosen not to impose federal rules and laws over the program for the sake of smooth and quick agreements with the provinces.

I concluded that when negotiating the terms of particular infrastructure agreements, the federal government had exercised "executive federalism"; in other words the executive — the PM and Cabinet — had selectively applied our rules and laws. This realization made me even more suspicious of the infrastructure program and raised further questions about the people who made the decisions about it. In Quebec the province claimed responsibility. In the case of the First Nations, the minister for Indian and northern affairs had selected which projects to fund. But what about in the rest of the country?

I decided to expand my investigation in several directions.

NOTES

1. Government of Canada, Canada Infrastructure Works MP Info Kit (Ontario version), June 1994, p. 4.
2. Richard Lestage, *CIWP Question* [e-mail], message to Colin Robertson, copied to Ross Hornby, October 15, 1997.
3. Colin Robertson, *Re: CIWP Question* [e-mail], message to Richard Lestage, Wednesday, October 15, 1997.
4. Later I would receive a copy of an e-mail written by Susan Fletcher at Treasury Board that stated, "According to the TB guidelines on Access to Information, we are required to consult with PCO on all records which we believe could be exempt under Section 14 (federal-provincial affairs) of the Access to Information Act." Susan Fletcher, *Re: ATI 135-9798-0094* [e-mail], message to Martine Berube, January 6, 1998.
5. Alan Leadbetter, Office of the Information Commissioner, Ottawa, [letter], June 2, 1998. Response to question from Jay Innes concerning participation of the minister's press secretary in the sign-off process of file #3100-11108/001. The following is an excerpt from the letter: "During the investigation we inquired into the participation of the minister's press secretary and other exempt staff in the

sign-off process. The press secretary does not have any lawful authority, under the TBS delegation order, to make decisions concerning Access requests. However, it is not uncommon for departments to include exempt staff in the review and sign-off process. In my view, as long as it does not result in delay, such a practice is not improper."

6. L. Denis Desautels, Auditor General of Canada, [letter], May 11, 1998. Response to letter from Jay Innes dated April 29, 1998.

7. Richard Fadden, Assistant Secretary, Treasury Board Secretariat, [letter], February 11, 1998. Response to letter from Jay Innes dated January 30, 1998.

8. Interview with Jacques Chagnon was conducted in French and translated into English for use in this book.

9. Interview with Claude Ryan was conducted in French and translated into English for use in this book.

10. Waheed Malik, Investigator, Office of the Commissioner of Official Languages, [letter], December 21, 1998. Response to complaint #0668-98-F10, filed by Jay Innes.

CHAPTER 5

Help Wanted

My efforts so far had convinced me that I wasn't going to have much luck finding answers to my questions if I continued to question federal bureaucrats, who often appeared to be jealously guarding government information within their Ottawa bunkers; the research would have to extend into provincial capitals and municipalities across the country. My strategy was to shift the focus away from the impregnable fortresses of our nation's capital and toward the grassroots, where I figured access would be easier and information more forthcoming.

I decided to do my bit to improve the country's dire unemployment situation by offering summer jobs to young Canadians interested in finding out how infrastructure spending decisions were made in their own regions. To provide an adequate cross-section of the population, economic activity and political representation in Canada, I chose to focus on the provinces of British Columbia, Alberta, Manitoba, Ontario, Quebec and Prince Edward Island. I contacted university professors and journalism schools in those provinces, spoke to friends and former colleagues and asked for suggestions to find suitably keen researchers. I also sent along a want ad defining the job:

WANTED:

Who: Investigative researchers for a television documentary examining a government spending program.

What: Conduct research on three to four projects, including site checks and pre-interviews of potential subjects who will appear in the television documentary.

When: Five to six weeks of full-time research in the summer of 1998. Work may spill over into the fall.

Where: Six provinces — B.C., Alberta, Manitoba, Ontario, Quebec and P.E.I.

Why: An examination of the Canada Infrastructure Works Program that I hope will help to understand the way government works — to find out where government decisions are made, who makes them and what is considered when making those decisions.

How: Research, take careful notes and put together an in-depth treatment of the story. Interview notes will be made and shared. Onus will be on the researcher to suggest visuals and setting for interviews as well as providing a background and a brief biography of each person to be interviewed. We will be relying on the call of the researcher as to whether the interviewee would be good on television.

Duties: Read and familiarize yourself with assembled articles for your province along with the stack of general-information articles provided. Focus on selected projects; find all parties who may have something to say about the project and conduct interviews. Find the decision makers from the municipal, provincial and federal governments, including Cabinet ministers, members of the management committees and former bureau-crats, for interviews. File regular progress reports.

The response was positive, although the word "infrastructure" may have frightened a few people away. Over the next few weeks we put a team of nine in place and solidified plans for filming interviews for the television documentary, which had been prophetically called *Secrets in High Places*.

I provided each researcher with newspaper accounts of various infrastructure stories from across Canada and a summary of my findings so far. I acted as research co-ordinator, holding down central command at home in Ottawa, drawing the researchers' attention to the questions I had already posed to so many people, warning them of the defence tactics employed by civil servants and encouraging them to advance the work in their own particular way.

As their individual stories began to take shape, I suspected that we had embarked on a unique study of a major government program which might, with luck, lead us to insights about the country that I could not have imagined when I began the project 10 frustrating months earlier. It was also around this time that the idea of creating a supplementary book, a written complement to the video documentary, began to develop. I sent this memo to the team:

> I would like you to keep journals as we are considering publishing a book as a companion to the television documentary.
>
> As I may not be able to use some of your discoveries for the documentary, I need you to take me with you in your weekly reports. I suggest that you each use your reports to detail whatever personal responses and commentaries you may have regarding your search. Each report should have a narrative structure that will let me know how your week has gone. Keep asking yourself what the events of the week have meant to you.
>
> You have the freedom to draw inferences from what you find and what you feel. Let the reader join you in your experiences and share the moments when you feel confused, excited, apathetic or unhappy. Give lots of details and highlight the most important information. It may help us develop the narrative for the documentary.

To sum up, create a map outlining where you have been, the doors you have knocked on and the responses you have received.

Portions of some of these reports and many of the researchers' letters and e-mails have indeed found their way into this book. Together with the excerpts from the interviews we conducted over the next few months, they chronicle the way in which we all came to understand the government — and the country — a little better than we did when we started. They add an extra dimension to this story of an ordinary Canadian's quest for answers and the insights that were gained along the way.

PART II

Bridging Out

"You've got to keep on top of your infrastructure. What happened in Canada is we got behind. Drastically behind. To the place where bridges were closed down. Where roads were pocked with potholes. Where underground systems were breaking up all the time."

Ron Hayter,
former Edmonton city councillor and president of the Federation of Canadian Municipalities, speaking on the Canada Infrastructure Works Program in 1998.

CHAPTER 6

Ontario

The researchers who investigated CIWP spending in Ontario were Lori McLeod, a recent journalism graduate from Carleton University, and Deanne Corbett, who was interning at Stornoway Productions for the summer before heading to the University of Southern California at Berkley to study journalism in the fall.

The major infrastructure project in Toronto, which also soaked up most of the city's CIWP money, was the building of the National Trade Centre, a project that will be discussed in detail in Chapter 13. Lori and Deanne weren't providing many reports about roads, sewers and bridges being built or repaired in the city. One of the stories that did emerge, and which had caused some controversy, involved the building of nine new daycare centres.

The province had submitted the application for the daycare centres, proposing that the federal government contribute $1 million from the funding available under the infrastructure program. Some media reports indicated that provincial and federal officials did not agree on this matter, with one journalist reporting there was wrangling going on behind the scenes. Nevertheless, in the fall of 1997 the daycare centres were given the go-ahead.[1]

Deanne found out how the dispute was finally settled by talking to Howard Moscoe, a Toronto city councillor who was also the chair of the Toronto Transit Commission.

DEANNE: *Moscoe certainly knows how to play the game. He kept me waiting out in the hall while he handled a few "important" calls. He also has his chair positioned so that he can see everyone who passes by his office, you know the sort of thing I mean. He's all dramatic gestures, and he said he'd never met a camera he didn't like. He seemed rather bemused when I introduced myself and said why I'd come. I thought the interview would turn out to be a dud, but I was surprised.*

Moscoe commented on the daycare issue with no prompting whatsoever, although I think he was surprised I already knew about it. The money allocated to save the nine centres didn't go through any sort of approval process. Moscoe said he had just put lots of political pressure on Art Eggleton, the minister responsible for infrastructure, and bingo! There was the promised money. Accountability? Forget about it. At least the money went to a worthy project.

Though Moscoe appears to be a bloodthirsty political animal on the surface, I think he has a heart of gold. He really cares about issues like social housing, and is trying to get the spotlight back onto that issue rather than on the "glory projects" which so often steal the limelight. I guess he messes around in the political muck because he figures if some good is achieved, it's all been worth it. But as to our search for cost-benefit analyses and accountability, he said quite simply to forget about it. The only cost-benefit analysis that is done, he said, is an analysis of the political costs and benefits.

The word "infrastructure" was beginning to take on new and colourful meanings.

Lori had uncovered the fact that more than $10 million had been spent building bocce courts in North York — a Toronto suburb and the nation's richest riding. (For the uninitiated, the game of bocce is a cross between lawn bowling and horseshoes and is very popular with Torontonians of Italian heritage.) This expenditure had earned the infrastructure program some not-so-flattering media coverage.

LORI: *Today I interviewed North York city councillor John Filion. He came out with guns blazing about the bocce courts. He said about half of the council formed an executive committee which then divided up all the infrastructure money, leaving nothing for some of the other projects.*

JOHN FILION: There were some meetings in North York to decide how to spend the infrastructure money. At one of the meetings I naively suggested that we come up with some sort of criteria, some rational way of determining which projects were most needed and how the money should be spent. I suggested that the staff review all projects and rank them according to need. There was absolutely zero support for that. People kind of looked at me like, "Where have you been to think that we do things that way?"

Our job as municipal politicians is to address local concerns. It wasn't really the local councillor's place to say, "We shouldn't have bocce courts."... If your residents are screaming for a bocce court, you get them a bocce court. If you need a community centre, you get them a community centre. There's nothing terrible about that. I'm not faulting any of the municipal councillors who managed to get bocce courts approved. They were responding to the wishes of their local residents, and that's what municipal politicians are supposed to do.

Basically whoever yelled the loudest, manoeuvred the best and stick-handled the thing through council got their projects to the top of the list. There was an art to it. There was certainly some political skill involved in getting your project to the top of the list. Some people are just better at working the process than other people.

At that time I wasn't especially good at working that process. As a result, a project that I very much wanted — a community centre that I thought would have come at the top of any sort of objective needs assessment — didn't get funded. My ward was the only ward in the city that didn't have a community centre. My first reaction was extreme anger. I remember being so angry I couldn't sleep. I was just furious that this project was pitched out and less worthy projects got the money. And some politicians were almost gloating about it: "See how we out-manoeuvred you?"

> LORI: *He was livid when it happened, and threatened to go to the media and tell them about it. To pacify him the committee members told him that the community centre project he wanted in his area would be built in the next year. They kept their promise and built his centre. Filion said he "sold out."*

JOHN FILION: Injustice tends to make me very angry. For a few days I was kind of plotting to correct this injustice. I was planning to make a big splash about the inappropriate use of the money and how it hadn't followed any kind of rational process. When it was clear that the process was, "Let's make a deal," I belatedly made a deal too. After talking to some members of council and some staff members, I thought the more prudent thing to do, since my objective was to try to get a badly needed community centre for my area, was to become part of the deal making.

What I got was a promise that the community centre that had been cut out of the infrastructure project would be approved a year later, through the regular budget. The councillors lived by the deal; that community centre just opened last month.

It's not a story that anybody has been very interested in, but there are two million stories like this in the naked city.

We also talked to Toronto city councillor Jack Layton about the bocce courts. He had a slightly different take on them, and on the infrastructure program:

Projects such as bocce courts are a very small investment in a small recreational facility, but typical of the media, they've decided to use it as an icon for how money was actually spent. I think that's really quite an unfair characterization of the program to do that. Number one because those projects were decided by the City of Toronto. They wanted to have a number of infrastructure improvements, and parks and recreation services are infrastructure improvements.

You tell me that a playground set of swings, for example, that's rusting and falling apart shouldn't be invested in as part of maintaining a city's infrastructure? I'd say you're wrong. It's just as important a part of the city's infrastructure, for the well-being of the citizens, as the roads. A bocce court is a facility for seniors, primarily eastern and southern European, to play sports. Had we been talking about lawn bowling, golf courses or other more typically Anglo-Saxon or North American kinds of sports and making those available, I'm not sure you would have had the same reaction. Frankly I find this reaction around the bocce courts to be pretty close to racist.

It seemed like Layton was missing the point. We weren't attempting to judge the quality of the projects, and we certainly had no intention of slandering Italian Canadians. We just wanted to follow the decision-making processes of the program so that we could understand how bocce courts qualified under a program supposedly created to fund core infrastructure.

We'll continue the Ontario story in a later chapter.

NOTES

1. Jack Lakey, "$1-million grant saves day-care spaces," *The Toronto Star*, September 12, 1997, p. A4.

CHAPTER 7

British Columbia

Our researcher in British Columbia, Leanne Hazon, already had a solid grasp on political life in Ottawa before starting work on this project. Like Lori, she was a recent graduate of Carleton's journalism program. Leanne had grown up in British Columbia and returned to her home in Richmond after she finished university.

As it turned out, her home province was also home to the country's most expensive *real* infrastructure project.

Construction of the Annacis Island secondary sewage treatment plant cost $206 million of the $675 million spent in British Columbia under Phase I of the infrastructure program. The sewage treatment plant is in the riding of Delta, B.C., which was held by Reform MP John Cummins.

According to the Treasury Board, Phase I of the program paid for 400 projects and created 9,000 jobs in B.C. In the first three years of the program 70 percent of all funds went toward water and sewage projects, including projects in Nanaimo ($13.3 million), Kelowna ($27.3 million), Vancouver ($26 million), Prince Rupert ($5 million), Kimberly ($6.2 million) and Fort St. John ($1.1 million).[1]

LEANNE: *I arranged to tour the Annacis Island second-ary sewage treatment plant. A sewage treatment plant would seem to fit into the category of traditional infra-structure even though it was actually a construction project, which is something above and beyond the $44 billion in repairs the country needed, according to the Federation of Canadian Municipalities.*

It's quite a large facility and the section funded by the infrastructure program is already complete. The plant now handles the sewage of 900,000 people in 14 municipalities.

During a tour of the plant I was told untreated sewage no longer pollutes the Fraser River, which flows into English Bay and is the longest salmon-spawning river in the world. My tour guide explained that there's a $300-million salmon fishery that depends on this river, and the estuary of the Fraser River is a very important breeding ground and a migratory stopping-off place for birds. There are literally hundreds of differ-ent types of other marine organisms that rely on the health of the river. All those factors made the plant an obvious choice.

My guide said he was willing to answer certain questions but he was a little nervous about doing a full interview, for political reasons. I asked him what he meant and he said the government sometimes took too long with the funding and the project almost stopped a couple of times while everyone waited for the money to flow. He chalked it up to politics.

Delays seemed to be a common characteristic of the program in B.C. As discussed in Chapter 2, the delays in announcing infrastructure grants had led to the assertion that Reform ridings had received less than those with Liberal MPs. Now we were being told that delays in gov-ernment payments nearly put a stop to the project. Leanne tried to con-tact federal and provincial public servants administering the program to find out the cause of the delays, but she reported that she was encoun-tering her own problems.

LEANNE: *I'm having trouble getting information from the different levels of government. As I'm looking for the number of projects already constructed and the ones under construction in the B.C. program, I called Western Economic Diversification (WED), the federal regional development agency in the West, which also administers the infrastructure program. I've been in contact with WED and they know I want to interview the people involved in the decision-making process, but I'm still waiting to hear back from them.*

I have also made calls to the B.C. Ministry of Employment and Investment (one of two provincial ministries in charge of administering the program).

I wanted to know more about the way the program was administered and whether or not politics may have played a role in this program. I have just come back from an interview with my hometown mayor, Greg Halsey-Brandt of the Vancouver suburb of Richmond (population 155,000). His knowledge of local politics was expanded to the whole region when he was chair of the Greater Vancouver Regional District (GVRD).

He said he liked the fact that the program allowed cities to speed up many of their capital building plans by a number of years, and that it saved money on things like roads and sewers because fixing them later costs more. While appreciative of some of the program's qualities, Mayor Halsey-Brandt was quite critical of its implementation and administration. He said sometimes the municipalities had as little as six days' notice to submit their lists of projects and that the selection process was bizarre, slow and inefficient. The mayor did not like the fact that municipalities were shut out of the selection process and that, amazingly, they were never given any selection criteria by the feds or the province.

GREG HALSEY-BRANDT: I get phone calls from Victoria and Ottawa saying, "There's some money left. Do you have any priorities?" And they have to know by 5:00. It's run politically; that's why it happens that way.

The normal way that we deliver programs, particularly capital projects, is to have lots of input from everybody and discussions about the priorities. You need between eight months and a year, by the time you conceive something, design it, go to tender and build it. At least that's the case here. Sometimes it takes several years to do a project.

So being given six hours' notice, or even two weeks' notice, puts us at a real disadvantage in terms of what's doable within these time periods. But we give them the information, it disappears into a black hole and we wait for the press release to come out to see who were the winners and losers. It depends very much on who's calling, whether it's Victoria or Ottawa, as to how they see those particular projects.

As mayor I made a couple of calls provincially and federally to get clarification of projects, decision timelines, how much money was available — that sort of thing. I could get answers to the harder questions like "How much money is left?" But I couldn't get answers as to why you chose this project over that project. I couldn't get answers on those.

As in Toronto, the word "infrastructure" had taken on some rather colourful definitions in B.C. The parameters of the British Columbia infrastructure agreement specifically allowed a certain percentage of the money to be used for projects that fell under a much looser meaning of the word. B.C. was the only province to have this exception enshrined in its contract with Ottawa:

The management committee shall develop appropriate guidelines, rules and procedures for the total allocation of the federal and provincial contribution such that 85 percent of said total amount shall go to the infrastructure projects related to local water, sewer and local transportation services, while the remaining percentage shall be allocated to other physical infrastructure projects also serving the provision of public services.[2]

The clause meant that 15 percent of B.C. infrastructure funds would be committed to any projects justified as "serving the provision of public service."

The government term for theatres and community centres was "non-traditional infrastructure," or "soft" projects. The terms were well chosen and politically smart because they shielded the true definition of the word, in effect disguising the fact that that roads and sewers were competing with theatres and conservatories for tax dollars, and avoiding the outrage that might result if the public actually knew how its infrastructure money was being spent.

In a collection of newspaper articles Leanne sent me, one reported on grants of $6.4 million for nine cultural and arts organizations. These included the Vancouver Playhouse, the Vancouver East Cultural Centre, the Fire Hall Arts Centre, the New Play Centre (which later became the Playwright Theatre Centre) and the Carousel Theatre.[3] Leanne started to look into some other "soft projects," like the Stanley Theatre ($3.9 million) and the Pacific Space Centre ($8.6 million).

LEANNE: *I visited the Pacific Space Centre on Wednesday. Considering it cost me $10.17 with a student discount, I can't say I was very impressed. It's neat and it's interesting but it's not very big and you can see almost everything in about an hour and a half. The most interesting part is a virtual ride to Mars and back. Kids get a huge kick out of it and it was fun, but it certainly wasn't worth $10.17. And if you want to try out any of the other virtual rides they offer, you have to pay an additional $4 per ride.*

I then toured the Stanley Theatre in Vancouver and met with Bill Millerd, the artistic managing director of the Arts Club Theatre Company. He's the man behind the conversion of the 1930s heritage movie theatre. Millerd told me why he feels the 15 percent funding for cultural projects is justified.

BILL MILLERD: I think the cultural facilities are absolutely necessary for the health of a community. It's not just about roads and sewers. Of course those are vital and necessary, but public facilities like the Stanley Theatre are part of the reason why we live in a community and enjoy the community. I feel that the federal government was very forward-thinking by insisting that 15 percent be devoted to these sorts of projects — because there really has been no money available for capital grants to concert facilities at either level of government for the last decade.

I think, from the politicians' point of view, they wanted projects, what I would call public projects, that had a kind of high visibility. And the Stanley Theatre suited that. I also got the impression that this was important in ridings where there was a Liberal federal politician and a NDP provincial politician, and fortunately Vancouver Centre, where the Stanley Theatre is located, did have that combination at the time.

> LEANNE: *Millerd talked about how helpful local Liberal MP Hedy Fry was. She really pushed for the theatre. They are having money problems now and went back to CIWP for more money in Phase II of the program. But no luck.*
>
> *I have called the assistant to Hedy Fry a number of times and I haven't heard back. When he finally did respond, we weren't able to fit an interview into her schedule.*
>
> *I also met this week with Vancouver city councillor George Puil, who is very interesting and articulate in his opposition to the government's funding of "soft projects." He said the entire process is too political and that all the money should go to traditional infrastructure, not theatres and space centres.*

GEORGE PUIL: The whole idea was to renew existing infrastructure because it was falling behind, and that wasn't done. And I think that's unfortunate. I think that certain MPs used it as a pork barrel. They said, "This is a project and it's going to happen in my constituency, and so it should be done." That wasn't the intent of it at all. The intent of it was for things such as sewer pipes and water and roads to be renewed. The political

reality is, these people have to get re-elected and so consequently they would want projects done, in their own constituency, that have a high profile. And sewers don't have a high
profile. I mean, who wants to cut a ribbon for the opening of a
sewer pipe? I don't.

LEANNE: *I finally spoke to the people running the
program for Western Economic Diversification. They
wanted me to ask my questions in a conference call
along with their provincial counterparts. I didn't
want to do a conference call because I wouldn't be
able to see their faces and gauge their reactions.
Sometimes a reaction gives an indication of other
questions to ask and when to probe deeper. If I couldn't
see those reactions, it would make it harder to do the
interview.*

*So I called a couple of other people from the man-
agement committee. They didn't want to do interviews
at all, even off the record.*

*Finally, when I did get the interview, the meeting
was absolutely pathetic. There were three of them: two
from the management committee and one of their communications people who was there to tape the whole
thing for their records.*

*They had a very suspicious attitude. They asked,
"Why are you doing this?" I think they were worried
that the federal government would get painted in a not-
so-flattering light.*

*They bypassed many of my questions by saying,
"We can't answer that" or "You'd have to ask the
province." Yet when I called a bureaucrat for the
province he told me, "Oh, couldn't WED answer that?
They should have known that stuff."*

*Today I reread that article Jay sent me, from 1994, stat-
ing that the government had given more money to
Liberal ridings than any of the other parties. Jay said
the government responded by saying there was an*

imbalance caused by delays in dishing out projects in B.C. and Quebec.

Then I spoke with Dave Rudberg, the chief engineer of the City of Vancouver, who told me something truly crazy about the program that might explain the delays in B.C.

It needs to be investigated!

It appears that cities like Vancouver, Surrey and Richmond were given bike paths that nobody asked for.

The municipalities are pissed off because, as Rudberg said, they were looking for hard infrastructure projects to help alleviate the deterioration of urban infrastructure. Rudberg also said they wrote several letters to Ottawa to complain because they really wanted hard projects. He said the federal minister responsible for the infrastructure program in B.C. even got involved. Minister David Anderson vetoed several proposed projects, sparking a feud between Ottawa and the province that resulted in an eight-month period in which no projects were approved.

There seems to be a lot of tension between the feds and the province. My efforts to discover more about this have been continually thwarted. It's like trying to get water from a rock, which, funnily enough, may soon be possible if it keeps raining here!

I don't like leaving a million messages for the same people and never having my calls returned. And these people don't even know what I specifically want to speak to them about, just that it has something to do with the CIWP.

I have run into a wall of silence erected by provincial and federal government officials. First of all the province's information officer for CIWP said he had never heard of any tensions between the federal government and the province. Everybody knew that there was tension. It was commented on by plenty of people from the municipalities, and it was in a number of newspaper articles. But he told me, "I don't know what you're talking about. There's no tension."

The tension is over the bike paths. Many municipalities got funding for them all of a sudden; but they were all saying, "We didn't ask for these bike paths."

As it turned out, the provincial government had taken the bike path applications from the municipalities under the Cycling Network Program (50 percent of which was to be paid for by the province, and 50 percent by the municipalities) and turned them into infrastructure applications.

So the provincial officials were funding projects for these municipalities and the bike paths were cheaper than other projects. The province was supposed to pay 50 percent of the costs of the cycling program, but under the infrastructure program it was paying 33 percent of the cost and saving almost 20 percent.

I spoke with Reform MP Chuck Cadman. He was elected in 1997 to represent the riding of Surrey North. Surrey got three bicycle paths it didn't ask for. Now the city is not getting money for a major artery it needs. The artery has been put on the back burner.

Cadman thinks it's a reasonable program as long as it's done fairly and not for political gain. Right now, he said, there are too many political strings being pulled. He can't put his finger on what exactly, but one example is the fact that Surrey didn't get its major highway connector.

So I talked to the mayor of Surrey, Doug McCallum, who is furious at the level of funding the city has received. He pointed out that Surrey is the 10th largest city in Canada, and the fastest growing in the nation, but Surrey only received a small portion of the money it asked for. The city currently has a population of 330,000, with another 1,000 moving in every month.

McCallum isn't happy that they didn't get funding for highways. He said there is so much traffic congestion in town that industries are moving out because they can't move their goods in and out of town fast enough. You should see what passes as a highway there: it's two lanes and runs right through town. McCallum thinks the whole process is political. He's so angry that he doesn't know if Surrey would even participate should there be another infrastructure program in the future.

DOUG MCCALLUM: It was interesting in Surrey that we got some money for bike paths, which we didn't even ask for. We got some money for something that wasn't a priority for us. That kind of shocked us.

We have no idea who is making the decisions about the program. Even now I couldn't pick up the phone and phone someone. I wouldn't have a clue who to phone. We've tried. We've written letters, but we still are not aware of who we could contact. That's one of the frustrating parts of the process. Anytime you're spending taxpayers' money, the taxpayers themselves want to know the process and want to know how their money's distributed. In this case no one seems to have an idea of how the money was disbursed.

There has been no accountability in this infrastructure process in B.C. It's disgusting. I'm a taxpayer and I'm disgusted with not being able to know how the process works, how the money's distributed or who's making the decision on my tax dollars. I think it's a great program. I encourage the federal government to continue with it, but they've got to bring accountability into the process. They need to be sure the decision-making process is well known and that all the players are at the table.

LEANNE: *On Tuesday Brad Fisher, bicycle co-ordinator for Surrey, and I went to look at the controversial paths. Nobody really seems to be sure what happened with the province's bike path program but as Fisher put it, it sounds like the provincial government "cheated." From what he said, the province took all the applications received under its cycling program and used them as*

CIWP applications. Fisher says the paths the municipalities received were in the plans; they just got them sooner this way.

Surrey got a total of $750,000 to build three paths.

I have asked for an interview with David Anderson, the senior Liberal in the province as well as the federal minister of fisheries and oceans. He has agreed, but his media guy is a little hesitant.

He asked me to send my questions ahead of time so he can have a look at them.

I also had a telephone interview with Norman Lee, who is with the Ministry of Employment and Investment and is the acting manager of the Infrastructure Works Program for the province. I've decided there's a language called bureaucratese. Bureaucrats are very good at talking their way around questions. Norman did shed some light on the bike path deal though. He says there just wasn't a lot of money to go around, so that's why a lot of cities got the bike paths. He said that the Ministry of Transportation and Highways did have the money for bike paths. It was a 50/50 program between the provinces and the municipalities. Obviously when the feds got involved they kicked in a third. The province did take bike path applications from a different program and turn them into CIWP applications, but Norman says that, contrary to what the municipalities claim, any project that was going to be approved under CIWP needed an environmental assessment. So each city would have been informed and could have chosen not to participate.

Personally I think that is a ridiculous way of looking at it. I mean, if it's bike paths or nothing, what's a city going to pick?

I finally did the interview with David Anderson. I started by giving him a bit of a forum to speak about how *great the program is and how well it's working now that the province has a good minister in B.C. who can work with the federal government. He described the program as he saw it.*

DAVID ANDERSON: All three governments are accountable for the process. The process was reasonably straightforward. It didn't create enormous bureaucracies and vast mountains of paper and innumerable meetings of bureaucrats to determine issues of priorities and rankings.

The program overall was, I think, a very good one, even with the difficulties we had in British Columbia.

In both the phases of the infrastructure program there were six or eight times as many projects proposed as we had money to fund. So six out of seven were unhappy because they didn't get their projects funded. That's one of the unfortunate aspects of a popular program. The more popular the program, the more people become unhappy because their projects are not accepted. The proposals came from all the municipalities. They were sorted out by the province, to be put onto a provincial priority list. We then approved what came forward. So the decision making really was municipal, provincial and federal.

There were some people who were not as pleased as they might have been. For example, Vancouver argued that they got far less than another community next door to them. Why? Because we took $220 million for the largest single infrastructure project in the country, to put into sewage treatment plants on the Fraser River, in another constituency. Don't tell me that was not a benefit to the entire Greater Vancouver region.

LEANNE: *Then I broached the subject of tensions with the province in the second phase of the program. Minister Anderson didn't go into much detail, but he didn't avoid the question.*

DAVID ANDERSON: In the second round, because of provincial priorities, they were insisting on things to do with buses and bike paths. We did have a number of decisions made which, in the eyes of the municipalities — and I think they're right on this — skewed the program toward provincial priorities. We tried to protect the municipal priorities as best we could because the federal government didn't have any great priority objective. We wanted to make sure we had the best municipal projects approved. The province had a slightly different approach and I'm not criticizing it — I'm simply saying, recording a fact, the province had the priority of transit for infrastructure.

I made a speech to the Union of British Columbia Municipalities a little over a year ago. I committed myself, to the municipalities, that if we ever sign another infrastructure program, it will not be with the province's ability to skew municipal priorities toward provincial priorities. That's not to say that the money wasn't well spent. It simply wasn't spent in accordance with what was understood by the municipalities at the beginning of the program, in terms of their priorities.

> LEANNE'S CONCLUSIONS: *Let's face facts: this is all politics.*
>
> *What's unbelievable to me is that the province was allowed to pick through the project applications first and weed out a lot of stuff that it didn't want. The provincial government picked those projects that it thought were viable, gave them to WED and said, "Here's what we think should be done."*
>
> *The municipalities were nowhere to be found at this point; they were limited to just sending in applications. How does that work, when the province didn't let the people who were paying 33 percent have a say?*
>
> *It seems slightly asinine to me.*
>
> *This was my first look at the government's management of finances, but I had an idea going in that I was going to find inefficiency and bureaucracy.*
>
> *I figure I got the municipalities to tell me why they weren't happy, and I got some idea of what they were complaining about.*

But often when I went to the provincial or the federal level to find out what decisions were made, who made them and why, I found this wall of bureaucrats who didn't want to talk.

I can only guess the bureaucrats didn't want to say anything because they were afraid they were going to get in trouble!

NOTES

1. *Canada Infrastructure Works: Phase 1, Approved Projects by Infrastructure Class and Province* [media release], Infrastructure Works Office, Treasury Board, December 18, 1998.
2. The Canada–British Columbia Infrastructure Program Agreement, February 18, 1994, p. 5.
3. Barbara Crook, "Two governments play Santa with $6.4M for arts," *The Vancouver Sun*, December 13, 1994, pp. A1–A2.

CHAPTER 8

Manitoba

A friend in Manitoba suggested I contact Anette Mueller, a journalism graduate from Red River Community College in Winnipeg. Anette (pronounced Anetta) was born and educated in Germany; when she was in her 20s she moved to Canada and worked as a radio producer before becoming a travel agent. She eventually returned to school, and later worked on a Winnipeg-based TV travel show — so she knew something about the on-camera world. Anette's open, European perspective, coupled with a healthy skepticism, managed to attract the attention of more than one politician.

> ANETTE: *I drove through downtown tonight to look at the new streetlights across from the riding office of Cabinet Minister Lloyd Axworthy. The infrastructure program paid $1.6 million for the "replacement of existing sidewalks with decorative paving, lighting, landscaping and plaza."[1] Sure improved the office view.*

When looking at the lamps I couldn't help thinking that governments are running the country like shopping addicts: rack up that old credit card, put an overdraft on the bank account until there is no more money to be spent.

It feels so ironic that I try to balance my bank account, try to live a lifestyle with my future in mind, while my share of the national debt (like anyone else's share) is growing because of pretty streetlights.

Earlier in the week I met Russ Wyatt, who is running for city council. His campaign promises a safe community and road repairs. He is really big on infrastructure, so he gave me a tour showing me a couple of streets in Transcona that are in desperate need of repair.

Wyatt said Winnipeg is an old city with sewer pipes dating back to the 1890s. The pipes are only held together by "Manitoba gumbo" — which is really just clay. The city, he said, is in a big mess because of overspending, during the past 10 years, on big, fancy projects. And now municipalities are in need of provincial and federal help.

He said there's nothing in the budget for infrastructure next year. The city will either have to raise taxes, cut services or increase the debt to address future problems. This situation is the result of shortsightedness and the attractiveness of projects that generate ribbon-cutting ceremonies (as opposed to projects like sewer repair, which generally don't get a lot of publicity). He quoted former councillor Rick Boychuk, saying visible projects, such as asphalt paving, are black gold during the three months before an election.

He handed me a beautiful list, assembled by Boychuk, of community centres funded under the infrastructure program.

There was $6 million for the expansion and redevelopment of the Ukrainian Cultural and Educational Centre; $3.75 million to construct a cultural centre for the Italian Canadian League of Manitoba; and $900,000 for the creation of a German cultural centre and sports entertainment complex. By my count, 29 community centres received infrastructure money in the province.

The politicians who were the big winners and received community centres in their ridings were Liberal MP Reg Alcock (Winnipeg South) with seven centres, Lloyd Axworthy (the federal Cabinet minister representing the riding of Winnipeg South) with four (the runner up) and Ron Duhamel (federal Cabinet minister representing Saint Boniface) with three.

I met with Reg Alcock, the MP for Winnipeg South, who must have realized some benefits from the construction and renovation of seven community centres in his riding using infrastructure money.

He says he wasn't directly involved in the decision-making process on strategic projects, but gave advice on which projects to fund or not to fund. Federal Liberal Cabinet minister Lloyd Axworthy and provincial Cabinet minister Eric Stefanson were the main actors.

I asked him how community centres were accepted as infrastructure projects and he told me that federal MPs in the Manitoba caucus decided to equally distribute the community project funds to the Italian, Ukrainian, Jewish and German communities after it was decided by Axworthy and Stefanson that all ethnic groups would receive the same amount.

I asked him why so many "soft projects" had been funded. He gave me a lesson on the importance of being precise. He said that such projects weren't soft projects but "local, small community projects," meaning that $750,000 was assigned to each federal constituency for "local, small community projects."

The project descriptions are so generic that I can't be sure what actually was funded. I've found that the traditional idea of hard infrastructure was pursued more *in the rural areas. Roads and sewers were actually repaired and maintained there.*

In the City of Winnipeg itself a large percentage of the funds went into community-type projects such as a dormitory for the Winnipeg Ballet and a facility at the Manitoba Museum for the Hudson's Bay collection of historical artifacts. There was also $1.25 million for the dredging of Lake Minnedosa for the rowing competitions for the Pan-American Games, which will be held in 1999. All these projects are great ideas, but why are they funded under infrastructure? What do they have to do with infrastructure? I really feel that the interpretation of infrastructure has been bent.

This morning I met with Diane Sacher, a support services engineer for Winnipeg's Water and Waste Department. The city has only just started to assess its sewer system. She showed me video footage from inside a sewer that revealed it was held together by that Manitoba gumbo, with a tree root cutting through it.

Sacher said that once the department expands the video program (which gives Sacher and her colleagues an inside view of Winnipeg's sewer system) the engineers will be able to identify a leak and fix it before the water washes away the soil, causing a sinkhole. Sacher hopes to prevent problems like what happened downtown last week when a corroded sewer caved in and swallowed a parked car.

My biggest surprise came today though, when Diane told me not a single dime of the CIWP money was used to repair the sewer system!

DIANE SACHER: There was some funding dedicated to flood relief, but not to actual sewer renewal. I personally feel that those were policy decisions. Those were factors that have nothing to do with the Water and Waste Department. The politicians have made some decisions based on some public pressure. The public was describing their needs, and the politicians responded in that way.

What we find in Winnipeg is that the public in the past has focused on water-main leaks when they were occurring. Now we're getting a lot of focus on pavement because that's something that they're driving on and seeing every day.

> ANETTE: *I had an interview this afternoon with the deputy mayor of Winnipeg, Jae Eadie. He is also the former head of the Federation of Canadian Municipalities. I was sure he would have a strong opinion about the direction the infrastructure program had taken. After all, it was the FCM that lobbied and started the ball rolling to get the infrastructure repaired. So why are roads collapsing in downtown Winnipeg? I was disappointed by his answer.*

JAE EADIE: There was criticism that some of the projects that were financed by the three orders of government were not what one would term "traditional municipal infrastructure." There's some validity to those criticisms. However, the Federation of Canadian Municipalities always said from the very beginning that any of the projects that are financed by the three orders of government have to recognize municipal government priority. So if, in a particular municipality, an arena or a fountain or a concert hall was deemed by the municipal government to be one of their priorities, so be it.

> ANETTE: *I find this complacency alarming. A report commissioned by the FCM claimed that every man, woman and child would have to pay $1,500 each for a total of $44 billion to repair and bring back the country's infrastructure to an acceptable level. Forty-four billion dollars! As the FCM sponsored the report, I thought its representatives would be a little more concerned. I get the feeling the program was hijacked. But by whom?*

91

Later in our investigation we interviewed the report's author, McGill University professor M. Saeed Mirza. He commented on the credibility of some of the municipal decisions made under the infrastructure program:

What has led to the municipalities' lack of credibility is the Federation of Canadian Municipalities survey, stressing needs and the infrastructure deficit. When they were given this money on a one-third-share basis, they saw it as manna from heaven, and they spent it on whatever they wanted. The result is that only about 40 percent of the total money was spent in renovating the infrastructure, and the remaining 60 percent was used for building some new infrastructure.

When a city's facility department, or the infrastructure department, goes to the municipal council to ask for money, saying, "Look, we have to renovate this road this year," the first question the council asks is, "Can it wait until next year?" And the engineer thinks about it, and they arrive at a consensus after some discussion that, yes, it could wait. It waits one year, it waits a second year, it waits a third year. Finally, five or six years from then, the deterioration has occurred to such an extent that one ends up spending five or 10 times the money one would have spent initially. Deterioration is like cancer — once it sets in, it grows at a very rapidly increasing rate.

ANETTE: *I called Carol Harvey from the Infrastructure Secretariat. She asked for a list of Stornoway's productions.*

I asked for specific information on projects and the way decisions were made. She said she didn't have any of the detailed information.

Twice I have been told that Jill Vaughan, the director of the Infrastructure Secretariat, could help answer my questions. When I finally got through she acted as her own media relations person and gave me a lot of flak. She tried to find out what our documentary is all about and what other provinces we are researching.

When I asked for a meeting she told me she'd look in her day planner and call me back.

I have finally had my trip to Mecca, the highlight of my week. I have just come back from a meeting with the almighty Jill Vaughan.

I thought the meeting was perfectly timed because she had just returned from her holidays. It was soon obvious that her relaxed state had quickly worn off. She was extremely stressed when I turned on my little tape recorder. Vaughan became very flustered: "I can't talk with that thing on." When I continued talking she shook her head and told me to turn it off.

I turned the tape recorder off and was only allowed to turn it back on after I had given her a copy of Stornoway's company history.

I told her that the purpose of this documentary was to help Canadians understand how politics works, providing information that can be used to understand other cost-sharing programs. She found the mission to be admirable and positive and she agreed that tri-governmental programs are probably the way of the future because (1) they reduce the load on the taxpayer, (2) they improve co-operation among the various governmental levels and (3) they offer a better appreciation of the involvement of different governments.

She also said all questions about the decision-making process have to be answered by elected officials! Help!

I decided to give Anette a hand in her search and send a clear message to the people administering the program in Manitoba that we were a legitimate team of researchers trying to make sense of this spending program. I called Carol Harvey and asked if I could file an Access to Information request for the minutes of the management committee meetings to find out how decisions get made. She told me the province had a new Freedom of Information and Protection of Privacy Act that was only a few weeks old, and she didn't think federal-provincial programs were subject to the act.

Tired of wishy-washy answers, I called the federal government's infrastructure office in Manitoba. On the first ring the federal government's main man picked up the phone.

Oliver Buffie, the federal co-chair and the assistant deputy minister for Western Economic Diversification, responded to my questions with short, matter-of-fact answers. When the call was over I checked my calendar to confirm that it wasn't April Fool's Day. The exchange went like this:

Buffie: Good afternoon, Buffie speaking.

Jay: Hi, it's Jay Innes calling. I'm a researcher in Ottawa and I am calling to try to get my hands on the minutes from the infrastructure management meetings. Would I have to make an Access to Information request?

Buffie: No, we don't have management infrastructure meetings.

Jay: Really?

Buffie: No

Jay: Mr. Oliver Buffie, infrastructure co-chair?

Buffie: Yeah ... but there's no official meetings where minutes are kept.

Jay: Really?

Buffie: Yup.

Jay: Is that standard procedure?

Buffie: Yeah.

Jay: Hmm ... because I have been able to obtain the minutes from all the other provinces.

Buffie: Well, hasn't ... uh ... none here. Sorry.

Jay: OK. Thanks a lot.

In the fall of 1998 Anette found out that there was going to be a ribbon-cutting ceremony to reopen the Assiniboine Park Pavilion Gallery. The art gallery was to become the home to, among other works of art, the 1930s painting of the bear that inspired A. A. Milne's Winnie the Pooh children's stories. While attending the ceremony to celebrate the $2.25-million renovation, Anette noticed a large plywood infrastructure sign that credited the federal and provincial governments but not the City of Winnipeg. She approached Winnipeg mayor Susan Thompson to ask why the city had not asked to be recognized for its contribution to the project. The mayor told Anette that the city had helped pay for the project with two subsidies, but these were not administered through the infrastructure program. When Anette pressed further, inquiring whom she could speak with to learn more about the project, the mayor sniped back, "Ask the powers that be."

Rather than back off her line of questioning, Anette took the mayor's blunt advice literally and approached Manitoba premier Gary Filmon — after the ribbon had been cut and the media had finished snapping all its photographs.

ANETTE: *Initially when I approached Mr. Filmon at the ceremony about a brief interview, he was willing to talk to me. When I tried to interview him again about 30 minutes later, he told me flat out that he knew who I was and that he wasn't interested in talking to me. Huh? What did he mean by "I know who you are?" I felt a cold shiver run down my spine.*

Mr. Filmon said he wouldn't talk to me because this opening was "a positive event." I assured him that I didn't have a negative attitude; I simply wanted to ask him a couple of questions.

If this pavilion was such a wonderful project, as stated during the opening ceremony, then why would Mr. Filmon not want to talk to me? I have to assume there must have been something that made him uncomfortable.

A little while later Mr. Filmon's communications officer approached me and asked me what questions I had for the premier. I said I wanted to know how this project qualified as infrastructure and who was accountable for the decision to fund it. Mr. Filmon finally agreed to an interview.

After this interview, there's nothing much that can surprise me.

ANETTE: First of all, the infrastructure program promised to repair roads, sewers, bridges. Today we're here celebrating the opening of this project. And there are, among others, seven community centres, bell towers, fountains and a baseball diamond that received infrastructure funding. How did these projects qualify for infrastructure money?

GARY FILMON: The infrastructure program was always more broadly based than just sewers, water and roads. It was always intended to improve the economic strength of a province and to contribute toward its ability to grow and prosper, and from our perspective we've invested in things that do that. Our investment here is about three quarters of a million dollars and it attracted over $10 million of private investment and created a site for tourism activity that will be one of the finest in Canada — and will probably become one of the two or three top sights for people in Manitoba and will attract people from all over the world. So that's the kind of multiplication factor that we look for. It's not just something that governments want to put all the money into and nobody else does. When we can multiply our investments as substantially as we do here, then we feel that we've done a great service for the people of our province with minimum use of tax dollars.

ANETTE: With a definition of infrastructure that's so broad, isn't it really difficult, or basically impossible, for a citizen to account for public spending?

GARY FILMON: I don't think so. Every citizen has the right and the responsibility to ask their elected representatives what value they got for each investment they make. And I'm quite prepared to examine critically every investment and tell the public exactly what they got from it, just as I've told you of investing three quarters of a million dollars and getting over $10 million of private capital invested into this project. I think that's a good return for our investment.

Anette was no longer a neophyte in public policy journalism. Her on-the-job education in the world of politics would continue the following day, when she conducted a scheduled interview with Finance Minister Eric Stefanson, the provincial minister in charge of infrastructure and one of the two men identified as the decision makers in Manitoba. She had made the initial contacts prior to the pavilion ceremony and had complied with a request from the minister's office to fax her questions ahead of time.

After the questions were submitted she was told that she would be granted a 30-minute interview the day after the pavilion opened. On the day of the ribbon-cutting ceremony she confirmed the details with the minister's office. Anette received a phone call early the next morning telling her that Minister Stefanson's schedule had changed and her interview had been cut from 30 minutes down to 10. The interview had also been moved from mid-afternoon to mid-morning. It crossed our minds that the short notice and limited access may have been punishment for crashing the premier's ribbon-cutting ceremony.

ANETTE: *I was given 10 minutes in the hallway outside the minister's office. Three members of the communications staff were there and watched me closely. During those 10 minutes I learned first hand that politicians and bureaucrats don't talk English or French, but something that can't be understood by an average citizen. For the most part Stefanson talked a lot without actually saying anything. However, I did find out who made the decisions in Manitoba.*

ANETTE: I've heard from two different sources that infrastructure decisions were made between yourself and Mr. Axworthy over the phone.

ERIC STEFANSON: Mr. Axworthy was the federal minister responsible, for the majority of time, on the infrastructure program. We met regularly and had reports prepared for our meetings. The final decision-making process was usually at a meeting with Mr. Axworthy and myself, but on occasion we would talk on the phone if we already had all of the background material and were able to make a decision. But the majority of decisions were usually made in meetings between Mr. Axworthy and myself, with our officials present and all of the documentation required to make the decisions.

ANETTE: *Cutting through a thick bureaucratic wall only seems possible when someone in a powerful position wants to help you.*

ANETTE'S CONCLUSIONS: *When I graduated from journalism school I got a phone call from Jay Innes about the opportunity to work on this project and I thought it was a really excellent chance to put my newly acquired skills to work.*

I'm interested in political events. I've seen different political systems. I thought it would definitely be a great crash course for me to find out about the current Canadian political system.

I didn't know what I was getting into. I figured it would be a lot of work in terms of asking a variety of people questions, but when I started phoning different governments, lo and behold, I found that people kept putting me off. They would tell me they'd get back to me, but they wouldn't. I couldn't get any answers and I didn't know why.

The municipal level was more interested in talking to me. It seemed most municipal politicians had little say about the overall decision-making process of the program.

Consequently they were eager to express their views and opinions and to seek recognition for their contributions.

I got few answers from the provincial or federal levels. I had an incredibly difficult time just talking to a minister and I was treated with suspicion, on the assumption that I had a preconceived slant. My biases only developed after I was sent in circles.

If I can't get straight answers to my questions, how can I understand government spending decisions? If I don't know how government decisions are being made, who does know? If no one knows, the political establishment can just continue working in a haze.

I felt like a failure and I questioned myself, asking, "Have I failed? Am I just a lousy researcher?" But no, I think I'm just a normal, average person, and I asked the questions everyone would like to know the answers to.

NOTES

1. Infrastructure Works Office, Treasury Board Secretariat, Canada Infrastructure Works Project List [work sheet on computer disk]. Master list of 12,628 Canada Infrastructure Works Projects from 1994 to October 31, 1997.

CHAPTER 9

Prince Edward Island

A friend who had worked with me on *Days of Reckoning* and who was now a CBC radio reporter in Charlottetown told me about his former colleague Jennifer Nunn. Jennifer had credentials as a journalist and was an inquisitive and experienced traveller, always in search of adventure. My friend felt she would be ideal for the project, so I hired her as our P.E.I. researcher. Almost as soon as she settled in to read the background files I had sent her, she began struggling with fundamental questions about the role of government in our lives.

> JENNIFER: *My first week working as a contributor on this project started with a crash. I was at my mother's cottage in Nova Scotia and awoke to the news that Swissair flight 111, with 229 people onboard, had gone down in the waters off Peggy's Cove near Halifax. Over the next few days I followed the search-and-rescue work on TV. I thought, this is why we pay taxes to the federal*

government: so the men and women who work in search and rescue are trained and ready to be there when the need arises.

I began to think about the other roles the government plays in our lives: building our roads, repairing our sewers and ensuring we have the water we need. These things may not measure up to the work done during a massive emergency, but they too are things that contribute to the quality of life we Canadians have come to expect.

When I think about the CIWP I question why the federal government felt the need to create a special program to do what our tax dollars are already supposed to provide. My next question is, did the three levels of government involved in this cost-sharing program select the right projects for the right reasons?

I have to say that many of the people I have spoken with so far are open and frank about the program. The only person I spoke with who was defensive was a local politician in a community where the infrastructure program money went toward building a bowling alley.

Rod MacNeil is only 43 but has been chairman of the Tyne Valley village commission for 21 years, so he knows how government works. He's seen the projects come and go and knows how to play the game to get what the community wants.

He wanted to know my "slant" on the story. I can't blame him for wondering if we are trying to criticize the project. Whenever you "look into" something like this, most people think you are trying to find problems. Once I explained that we just wanted to see how the decisions are made and how the process works he came around a bit, even inviting me to come up and see the bowling alley. I plan to do just that later this week.

I went to Tyne Valley to see this project that is described as a "community centre," but basically is a bowling alley. The *municipality decided not to submit an entire list of projects to the infrastructure committee because the local firemen's association wanted to get money to add a bowling alley to the local club. The municipal leaders figured if they put in a big list, then the powers that be may have chosen something else. And Tyne Valley politicians felt they needed the bowling alley. In the end the firemen got $300,000 in infrastructure funding.*

What's interesting here is that this is a non-profit group that received the money and the project has actually created two "real" jobs. I like that part. Many of the other jobs I've looked at are the non-specific types that don't last in the long term.

The strategy of only applying for one project was obviously the right one because the nearby community of Miscouche also had an interest in building a bowling alley. Miscouche included it in a list of other projects and the bowling alley lost out.

I met Stephen Ellis, the past president of the Tyne Valley Firemen's Club and the major force behind the project. With him was bowling alley manager Barb Broome, whose job was created as a result of the infrastructure funding. Both believed the survival of the community relied on the conversion of the local watering hole into a family centre that boasted the only 10-pin bowling facility on the island.

STEPHEN ELLIS: I'll put it to you this way. Would you build a road to nowhere? I mean, you have to have someplace to go.

BARB BROOME: We definitely need our roads fixed, and we definitely need sewers in, but we also need projects like this because the money that's made here generates back into the community. Most people have heard of us now, you know: "Yes, I've heard of Tyne Valley because of the bowling centre."

STEPHEN ELLIS: I'm pleased that they had a broad enough view of it to include us, but how we managed to get included into it? I don't understand the process, and I don't even claim to understand it. Is it infrastructure? For most people, they say infrastructure is sewer lines, water lines, roads. For a rural community like us, that's very limiting. Our opinion is, for our rural communities to survive we basically have to provide services. We have to make it a place where people want to live.

BARB BROOME: And eventually they'll fix the roads.

I spoke with Bobby Morrisey. He's now in Opposition but spent many years in the provincial Cabinet. He's always been considered a real backroom dealer who knows how to get things for remote rural areas.

Morrisey said he won't apologize for delivering to his area. He believes the money and projects are important to keep small communities going. He addressed the question of using infrastructure money to build ball fields and bowling alleys. To him that's part of keeping the community going, keeping the people happy, and that's part of being a politician.

While I was on the road this week I also spoke with a contractor who did most of the work for the City of Summerside's infrastructure improvements. Walter Real is the owner of a local construction company and he said the industry was in hard times when the program was announced and that without the program he wouldn't have been very busy and wouldn't have hired the 40 extra men he did, although most of these jobs were temporary, short-term positions.

Real said from his point of view the money should only have gone to roads, sewers and water; he also said that the program wasn't intended to hand out political plums but in some cases it did. When I asked him to explain, he said it's just known that these things happen.

The history of Charlottetown predates Confederation, so, as Jennifer found out, the city had a long list of traditional infrastructure projects that were eligible for funding. She met with Clifford Lee, a city councillor and the chairman of the public works committee, to discuss some of the city's new projects, like the road down to the wharf and the new storm sewers, which were built to end the flooding problems in older sections of the city.

Near the end of the conversation Lee warned that some communities that used their infrastructure funds to pay for non-traditional projects could become dependent on government subsidies and find themselves in need of more help:

> In the long run I'm not sure that those communities will be able to sustain the operations of those buildings. I think they are going to be coming back in a couple of years' time looking for somebody else now to assist in subsidizing that community hall because it's too big. It just costs too much to operate the building, and there's not enough people in the community who use the building on a regular basis to pay the costs associated with operating. I'm not sure a lot of that "down the road" approach was looked at.
>
> I'm not suggesting that a project wasn't worthy to be done. I'm wondering aloud about the long-term viability of the project. I just don't believe that some of the projects will last into the future. I think the communities or organizations, in a lot of cases, that acted as the agents for some of these buildings will find, unfortunately, that they're not able to operate them.
>
> From my perspective I think the program just worked well for the province with projects approved from one end of the island to the other. I guess we can all look at some of them and question whether some of the projects make sense, but I guess only time will tell.

JENNIFER: *I visited the community of Alberton, where the secretary to the town's chairman told me about the sewer and sidewalks that Alberton put in. The sidewalk* *that I saw cost $60,000 and leads to an outer area of the village. There's not a great deal of traffic on it.*

One example of a funny and frustrating response from a government employee came when I asked the secretary if I could look at the folder in her hand labelled "Infrastructure Program." As soon as I asked for the folder, she pulled it back: "Why, what good would it do?"

I couldn't believe how nervous she was. I said it wasn't a big deal, I just thought it would be interesting to have a look and see if anything caught my interest. She said it was just clippings and nothing interesting. She obviously wasn't comfortable letting me see it, so I didn't push.

Georgetown is a small town with a fish processing plant that has shut down and reopened more times than people care to remember. It has a fairly active wharf, and in the summer it's a theatre town. It has a colourful former mayor, Charlie Martell, who kicked up some dust during the program's early days.

The town works hard to get what it gets. It received about $500,000 in the first phase of the infrastructure program. The money was used primarily to put an addition on the municipal building and fire hall, repair and upgrade some parks and improve street drains and sewer lines.

What's interesting is that Martell wasn't very happy about the process by which the municipalities got the money. In the first phase he was told that there was some money left over and the town should reapply for extra projects. He heard the town was getting another $300,000, but it only got $150,000. Martell figures the amount changed when it got to Ottawa. He thinks the money was redirected somewhere else.

Martell said the overall program is worthwhile. What municipality wouldn't want to pay 33¢ on the dollar to get what it needs? But he said the system of dividing the money isn't fair and wondered why Ottawa should have all the say when it only puts in one-third.

CHARLIE MARTELL: I went down to Charlottetown to complain about that, but I never did find anything out. I didn't want to make too many waves because a lot of times the politicians and the top bureaucrats get mad at you and a lot of them have long memories.

There probably was politics involved in a lot of the decisions, but you know, that's living in Prince Edward Island. If you fellas find out how the decisions were made, I wish you'd get back to me.

I spent a somewhat frustrating hour on Friday with George Likely, the director of policy and administration for the Department of Community Affairs. I know George through his wife, Jenny, so we aren't strangers. But even with this connection I could not cut through the defensive barrier which I find most government employees throw up the minute they are asked to explain or — God forbid! — defend the actions of their department. He refused to allow me to record the conversation.

In a nutshell, he strongly believes the program was worthwhile and beneficial in that it helped the communities get what they badly needed. He talked about the decline of infrastructure in many rural areas and said that the cost to address the problem was too high for the municipalities to fund on their own. He said 80 percent of the work done on P.E.I. was for traditional infrastructure projects and that the review committee, the committee that examines all project applications before passing them to the management committee, had traditional infrastructure in mind when it started reviewing the proposals.

However, he didn't deny that some money went to areas not traditionally considered to be infrastructure.

106

But he said those things were also beneficial. If a community made a ball field or a fire hall its top priority, then why would the committee argue with it? Besides, he said, some communities may not have been able to come up with the money for a larger infrastructure project, so they chose to do something else.

George said the committee didn't want to get into projects that could end up costing the province money in the future. He did say that if the committee came across a project that the federal government could fund some other way, the project was usually rejected and the applicants told to seek alternative funding. That way the money was available for another project.

As for political pressure, he said there simply wasn't any. He said no one ever came near the committee to pressure it to approve one project over another, and that the goal was to spread the money around the province so that all communities felt they'd benefited from the program. But that's not political pressure, he said, that's just the nature of politics: "Is it politics or just common sense to spread the money around?"

When I asked him if he could provide me with minutes about the discussions around an individual project, he said the committee didn't keep minutes of its meetings. It didn't record how a decision was made. Committee members were told they only had to document the fact that a meeting was held and who was in attendance.

After our interview we discussed the attitude of some government employees toward people like me who have questions about what is done within government. I've always been the kind of person who can relate to both sides of the story. I understand that people always have a reason for what they do, and I believe that when you start asking people to account for themselves or their employer, they automatically start thinking about saying the right thing and protecting their jobs. That's understandable, but it can be annoying.

George said that many government workers are defensive for a reason. He felt that some people, myself included, might be trying to find the negative side of the story. I assured him we were simply trying to follow the process of how federal money is spent and determine how the decisions are made to fund one project over another.

I did manage to speak with one woman who was on one of the committees. She said she had the feeling that when the federal representatives went from one meeting into another, all of a sudden changes were made to the project list. But that's as far as she would go. She wasn't even comfortable saying that.

So far, no one I've found who was involved behind the scenes has been able to give me a great deal of insight. They've explained the criteria for choosing projects, but not the rationale.

Jennifer, unlike the other researchers, couldn't apply officially for any information on the infrastructure program in P.E.I. because the province does not have legislation similar to the federal Access to Information Act. But she found two people, Charlie Campbell and Leo Walsh, who had been intimately involved with the program and, much to her surprise, were willing to talk.

Charlie Campbell was the deputy minister of intergovernmental affairs for P.E.I. and had represented the province in negotiating the federal-provincial infrastructure agreement. He had been retired for three years when Jennifer travelled to his home in the Charlottetown suburb of Stratford. The bonus for making the drive, Mr. Campbell promised, was that Jennifer could see the rarely used sidewalks in his community that were funded through the infrastructure program.

JENNIFER: *Campbell said the fact that the infrastructure program was a pillar of the Liberal's 1993 election platform, which promised quick job creation and smooth relations between governments, set the tempo for the whole program. After the Liberals won the 1993 election they created a special task force under Art Eggleton, the minister in charge of infrastructure. The usual federal line departments were cut out of the process so that the task force could avoid the slow pace that usually characterizes the negotiations that go on between the two levels of government in federal-provincial dealings.*

The first meetings between P.E.I. and Ottawa were held in November 1993, and the federal-provincial agreement was signed on January 21, 1994. Mr. Campbell told me that he appreciated the speedy process and wondered why all governing can't be as quick and efficient.

CHARLIE CAMPBELL: The agreement called for things to be fast-tracked in order to create an immediate profile as a government of action.

The speed with which it happened was not unusual in terms of the new federal government's objectives in three areas. One was to assist municipalities in putting needed infrastructure in place. Another was the economic and social objective of trying to create some new jobs, and create some economic industrial activity. And obviously the government also had some political objectives.

JENNIFER: *The proposal from Ottawa was that the money should be divided based on each province's share of Canada's population. Campbell argued that, since the program emphasized job creation, the provincial share of total unemployment should be factored in as well. Ottawa agreed to add the two numbers and divide by two. This increased P.E.I.'s share of the total infrastructure money from 0.5 percent to 0.6 percent, which translated into a total of $42 million.*

Then, in another clever move, by reminding Ottawa of the long winter season on the island, which limits the number of months available for cementing sidewalks and laying down sewer and water pipes, Campbell and his colleagues convinced the feds to extend the life of the program from two to three and eventually five years. But keeping up the rapid pace of the program was still Ottawa's top priority, followed closely by its obsession to be given due credit, as Campbell explained.

CHARLIE CAMPBELL: It was indicated within the agreement that there had to be a high degree of signage, with the result that, as the agreement got carried out, there were lots of red-and-white signs in communities all across the country six months or a year prior to the 1997 election. As political strategy it was masterful.

JENNIFER: *Mr. Campbell defended the decision to include community hall construction and renovation within the parameters of the program on the basis that those projects often created more jobs at home than did traditional projects, which usually relied on equipment from outside the province.*

CHARLIE CAMPBELL: A small community might get $50,000 toward its project. But you have to keep in mind that probably 80 percent of that project would have been spent on the island, whereas most large infrastructure projects tended to be 50 percent labour, 50 percent equipment and so on. In the case of a community hall, not only the labour but the materials could be island-produced, and all the expenditure would remain in the province. So it would rank high according to the criteria.

JENNIFER: *Campbell was a little more realistic about the municipal reaction to long-term economic benefits.*

CHARLIE CAMPBELL: It was as though the municipalities were invited to a dinner and they got the appetizer, but they didn't know what was coming next and they didn't really know what the main entrée was going to be. Everybody is interested in getting the here-and-now project and doesn't necessarily look to the future. There is a tendency for people to say a bird in the hand is worth two in the bush.

Leo Walsh was the vice president of the Atlantic Canada Opportunities Agency (ACOA), the federal regional development agency in Eastern Canada, and one of two federal public servants on the management committee for P.E.I. during the time of the infrastructure program. When Jennifer interviewed him he had already left the federal public service.

> JENNIFER: *Leo Walsh told me that he called the ACOA office to tell his former employer he had agreed to an interview and asked if the agency had any problem with his making comments about the infrastructure program. He said the person he spoke to chuckled before telling him ACOA didn't give a damn.*
> *What I find striking about Mr. Walsh's interview is his recognition that short time frames affected the program from its inception right through the selection process, and that rules and decisions were made on the fly.*

LEO WALSH: I want to emphasize that this program was in the embryonic stage. It was evolving, so we had no protocol to be guided by. The application process was not well defined initially because there were no hard-and-fast guidelines about where, who or what.

Someone would express interest in a project, and then we had an informal exchange of information to get a sense of what kind of demand was out there and what kind of projects we might be looking at during the course of the program. I think the program life was never thought to be long. I always sensed that this was to be done quickly and that it would end. There was an urgency for people to get their projects moved forward because there was not a long window here.

When processing applications we had to try to reach a consensus because there were three levels of government involved in making the decision and nobody had a veto. We went by perhaps a sense of value or support that could be attached to each project, and then we worked to prioritize. The important thing was to get all parties and all partners agreeing on a priority. It was that exchange of attitudes that guided you.

It was subjective — certainly some of it was — but there was also financial analysis and rigour and a measure of the benefits — whether political, social or economic. These things were all considered and in the end I would say perhaps 98 percent of the decisions were very good.

Benefits are certainly hard to measure. What is the value of having certain amenities or facilities or improved sidewalks? There is no hard, cold measurement to determine the social value of a public project in a community.

What is the value of fresh, pure, clean municipal water when you have a high concentration of homes in an area where there is potential intrusion of waste and high bacteria counts? It's difficult to measure the economic value by itself, so it's a combination of factors that help you to make an informed and defendable decision.

I was part of a management group that evaluated projects but I didn't have a veto, nor was it intended that anybody have a veto. I want to emphasize that consensus was important. Everybody had to agree, so we did our evaluation and moved it up to another level. Project approvals were brought forward and agreements were signed. I couldn't comment on who ultimately decided because that was beyond my level of authority or involvement. Ultimately a decision was made. That's the way democracy works.

In the last days of her research an unexpected gift was delivered to Jennifer's door. It was one of the first copies of the 1998 Report of the Auditor General of Prince Edward Island.

JENNIFER: *I've just received a copy of the P.E.I. auditor general's report. There are about six pages on the infrastructure program. In the report the auditor general mentions the fact that no minutes were kept in the meetings and there's no way of discovering why one project was chosen over another. You would think that when you're spending millions of dollars, you would record the reasons why you've chosen to spend them.*

I just assumed that when you're working in that kind of a committee structure you would keep minutes. I was surprised that nobody seemed to think that the infrastructure committees should have — people keep minutes of meetings at the most basic community level. And nobody involved with CIWP seemed to be overly apologetic — not a lot of mea culpas — that this kind of record keeping wasn't done. Only starting in May 1997 were minutes kept, but up until then, nothing.

The auditor general's report also points out that the accounting procedures behind the whole infrastructure program were fairly sloppy. There were times when invoices were submitted twice and paid out twice. Nobody caught that. And then when someone did realize it and asked for the money back, the municipality asked if it could keep the money and spend it on something else. And that was approved.

In the report the auditor general said he couldn't find out why three private projects were selected: "There were no explanations as to why these particular projects were given priority over other strictly public sector projects which were rejected."[1]

The other point the report makes is that jobs were supposed to be created as a result of this money being spent. But nobody really went back to see if those jobs actually did get created. Or even to see, in some cases, if the work was actually completed.

The report is really good, but unfortunately the auditor general won't do an interview. He rarely does interviews and the report has yet to go to P.E.I.'s public accounts committee, so he's got good reason to decline.

JENNIFER'S CONCLUSIONS: *There were times when I felt that I had broken through the barrier of token responses and started a real discussion on the way the government works. Sadly, the most open conversations were with the people who had left government and were no longer involved in making decisions.*

Earlier this week I listened to an interview with Premier Pat Binns. During the discussion he referred to plans to turn P.E.I.'s waste-distribution system over to private industry. He said the private sector can usually do things better and more cost efficiently than the government. I wanted to scream, "WHY?"

Why can't the government operate efficiently while still maintaining the services we need, from clean water to the search-and-rescue crews who worked around the clock after the Swissair crash? I certainly don't believe the bottom line should be the dollar value, but if the government doesn't waste, then there's more money to help the average Canadian have a better life. It just makes sense.

It's important to continue to ask questions and care about what the government is doing at all levels. And we have the right and the obligation to always hold it accountable, not just at election time.

The ultimate responsibility for accountability in the infrastructure program lies with the federal government. That's really where the responsibility is. I phoned all the members of Parliament for the island. I explained to their staff members who I was and what I wanted. I always asked them to have the member of Parliament call me back. I never did get to speak with any of the four MPs. They never even bothered to call back. Maybe the politicians don't call back because they think the person or the problem will just go away: "If we don't rush back, maybe we

*won't have to answer." Or maybe they just haven't
given it that much thought.*

NOTES

1. Office of the Auditor General of Prince Edward Island, "Chapter 6:
    The Infrastructure Program," *Report of the Auditor General to the
    Legislative Assembly, PEI, 1998* (Charlottetown: Office of the
    Auditor General, February 20, 1998) p. 35.

CHAPTER 10

Quebec

Brigitte Pellerin, a freelance journalist and columnist, was one of two researchers in Quebec. Brigitte holds a law degree from Laval University. For our project she worked out of her home base in Quebec City.

Our other Quebec researcher, Philippe Forest, was an aspiring playwright and director. Perhaps a rather unconventional choice for this sort of work, but I thought his artistic background and his familiarity with Montreal would be strong assets.

> BRIGITTE: *This morning I called the ministry responsible for handling the infrastructure program to ask for a copy of the project listings in Quebec. The person I spoke to said the ministry would send the list by express post. Then I asked, "Well, do you have anything else?" The reply was, "No, sorry, this is all we have." Whenever I called after that I didn't get any*

answers, or when someone did pick up he or she would just say, "Well, we'll call you back." But no one ever did.

I did speak with Maurice Boucher from the Ministry of Transportation about the application process. He said that, for the ministry's part, the projects it wanted had already been on the shelf, almost ready to go, and were waiting for a budget, that's it. So the projects the ministry sent to the committee were almost all accepted because of that. He also pointed out that the time frame played a great role in the selection process. Because everything had to start so fast, the committee did not want to argue over disputable projects. The applicants wanted the money that was available at that time and so played by the rules.

PHILIPPE: *I called City Hall today to find out whom I might speak to for further information concerning CIWP in Montreal generally. I was transferred to the office of former mayor Jean Doré, who transferred me to someone in the municipal archives, who transferred me to someone in communications, who said someone would call me back.*

I called the Ministry of Municipal Affairs to get a list of projects that received infrastructure money. The minister was not available. The woman on the other end of the line referred me to a Mr. Roy, who told me that the ministry deals with municipalities only and that such matters are confidential and cannot be divulged. We exchanged courtesies and hung up. Afterward I wondered at my lack of resistance. After all, I'm not demanding government secrets.

BRIGITTE: *Before going any further let's get something straight. It is virtually impossible to get any interviews in Quebec where the interviewee answers simple questions in a simple manner. Forget it. That's just not the francophone way.*

It's very hard to get straight answers to simple questions. I have to go there, act nice (smile!) and do my share of chitchat before I can start getting serious. Sometimes I have the feeling I am trying to seduce them.

I went to the Ministry of Municipal Affairs, to the Ministry of Transportation, the offices of the Parti Québécois, the provincial Liberals, former ministers, and they kept playing tennis with me. I was the ball.

Every now and then I can talk to somebody who is there and who has to know something, but most of these people are not willing to speak openly and frankly. Or maybe they just can't, I don't know. I have the feeling that I am trying to catch a fish with my hands.

PHILIPPE: *From the very beginning I was told that there would be obstacles. Told very matter-of-factly about the difficulty I would have getting information. I understood clearly what I had been told, I think. Just days into this work and already I have stumbled into a forecasted loop. A harmless fall, a small drop and hook. I am where I started, with this difference: understanding has made room for distrust. Physical distrust, like eating a bad clam. Maybe I am too sensitive.*

I called Jacques Laberge, public works engineer. Laberge is not aware of an annual assessment on infrastructure. I asked him how then does he determine infrastructure needs? He said that when citizens complain, the town checks things out. If something needs fixing quick, the people at the Department of Public Works fix it. If not, they wait.

BRIGITTE: *I have spent a lot of time talking to officials, bureaucrats, politicians, MNAs, you name it, and I've tried to understand the way they think. I tried to walk in their shoes for a while and see things the way they see them. I finally said to myself, "You're getting nowhere like this." Then I had a crazy idea. I thought that this might have something to do with George Orwell's idea*

of Newspeak — a new vocabulary, with new words car-
rying new meanings. So I decided to try to speak like
them, to act as if I were a member of this club, as if I
were somebody who spent a lifetime trying to under-
stand their logic. They liked it: "Hey, she speaks like us.
She knows about it, she understands."

After several conversations I reached the conclusion
that they don't understand everything they say. It's a
mystery to them too.

While trying to find out how many of Quebec's 2,616 projects targeted Montreal's roads and sewers, Philippe, like the other researchers, discovered some that didn't seem to fit the conventional definition of infrastructure, including tennis courts, churches and synagogues, and a new home for the Montreal-based circus Cirque du Soleil.

The world-renowned Cirque received $4.8 million from the federal government and the same amount from the province. Both grants were put toward a $14-million building to accommodate "circus training and production facilities." According to the federal government, this project would create 235.7 jobs.[1] Who got stuck with 0.7 of a job?

Media reports claimed that the infrastructure subsidy wasn't the end of the government's goodwill: the City of Montreal provided the land for the building at one-third of the market price.[2]

Another big winner in the infrastructure lottery was the very successful Intrawest, the company that runs Mont Tremblant and several other ski resorts, including Whistler in B.C. The media reported that the federal and Quebec governments would each give Intrawest $5 million to help it expand its Mont Tremblant resort. The money was used for roads and sewage systems inside the resort. In response to the media attention that resulted from this project, Intrawest chief executive Joe Houssian seemed to downplay the size of the subsidy: "At the rate we are spending money these days [$4 million a week] that $10 million will be gone in two and a half weeks."[3]

PHILIPPE: *Today I toured Montreal to look at some*
projects that received "infra money," if only to get a

concrete idea of what the money was used for. I walked by the Outremont Theatre. There is a fence in front of the theatre to prevent people from seeing inside its big windowpanes. One can peek through the fence, though, without much difficulty. There are wires dangling from shoddy ceilings and hardhats and tools scattered all over the place. It looks as though the workers have all gone to lunch.

The surrounding fence has been decorated and painted by grade-school kids. This fence could serve as a striking metaphor for concealment and deception. The fact that it has been painted over by children, who represent innocence, leaves me with a bad taste in my mouth and a feeling of foreboding.

I spoke to my cousin, an Outremont resident who is connected to the youth wing of a political party, about the theatre. He tells me a lot of money was lost and it's an ugly story. I will keep searching to find out details about the ugliness.

I have heard from a former Outremont resident that the story "L'Outremont" is filled with "déceptions and pots de vin." Money is said to have disappeared and work during reconstruction is said to have been poorly done.

This is all hearsay, but I smell a rat. I will read council minutes and meet with municipal councillors and then proceed from there.

I sat down and read the minutes of the city council meetings during which the Outremont Theatre was discussed. These minutes cannot be literal transmissions; they contain significant lapses and miscommunications. It seems to me that they lack content. I noticed that there are missing links in the dialogue and a general absence of clear topics, but simple actions are described with the finest accuracy — people get up, leave, come back. I wonder at the waste of time and paper. What kind of commitment to form *compels these morons to re-create the dullest, most insignificant details of the municipal politician's life? Dead men fall out of windows and politicians read themselves to sleep.*

But by reading municipal council minutes from 1994 to 1996, it became clear to me that the project was unrealistic from the very beginning.

The municipality pulled the plug on the project in March 1996 when it realized more than $1 million worth of work had been done without municipal council's approval. Council accused the construction company doing the renovations of either having withheld information, or of having falsified information concerning costs and overruns.

I have tried to speak with members of municipal council, with little success. Only Jacqueline Clermont-Lasnier agreed to speak with me, and considering the ongoing legal inquiry into this project by the Commission municipale du Québec, there was very little she could say. Some of the councillors I have tried to reach have already testified before the commission, but still refuse to call me back.

René Faribault, councillor and deputy mayor in the summer of 1995, spoke to me very briefly, admitting to internal squabbling and cost overruns. He assured me that the outcome has not had any negative effects on Outremont taxpayers. He added that if I wanted more information, I should wait until the commission has completed its process.

The current mayor of Outremont, Jerome Unterberg, did call me back last week. He was very friendly. He said that the project was not supposed to be done in a "fast-track" method. Rather, he claimed, entrepreneurs had more than four months between the time they were hired and the time the actual work got started. Four months to re-evaluate feasibility plans does not fall under the category of "fast track," he said. He thinks the project was — is

— a very good one. Unsurprisingly, he accused entrepreneurs of negligence and dishonesty. He applauded the CIWP and said he wishes there were more programs like it.

Jacqueline Clermont-Lasnier was an Outremont municipal councillor until 1996. She sat in opposition when the infrastructure program was introduced. (By the way, in Quebec, municipal politicians are affiliated with political parties). For eight years she was the councillor in charge of public works. I asked her what happened with the theatre. Apparently there was a petition of 3,000 to 4,000 signatures put forward in favour of buying and restoring the theatre. Much of the push came from retailers on Bernard Street. They hoped it would increase business. The town is suing companies that worked on the project and the same companies in turn are suing the town. That's all she could say about it, as she has been summoned to speak before the commission examining the controversy.

She said some of the sewers in Outremont are old and made of wood, and she expected that the sewers would be a priority for infrastructure spending.

JACQUELINE CLERMONT-LASNIER: Personally I never understood the choice. It was all politics. I protested in chambers. I think it is not the city's business to get involved in the entertainment business. There were political promises, and a petition with 3,000 to 4,000 signatures was circulated. It certainly was not residents of Outremont. Retailers on Bernard Street hoped it would bring them more customers. But frankly, when you go to the movies you don't go shopping and bring your grocery bags to the cinema! So it was purely political. And I thought that when the project was to be submitted to the governments it would be rejected. To my great surprise, it was accepted.[4]

PHILIPPE: *How can one grasp that which constantly denies its origin? When it comes to the infrastructure program in Quebec, tracing an idea from the beginning to the end seems practically impossible, given the dimension and complexity of the political machine in question. The problems of individual accountability pale before those of systemic accountability.*

The system conceals individual personalities under an impersonal rationality. For example, in the case of the Outremont Theatre, each councillor I spoke to referred me to another councillor or to a municipal administrator or to a public works officer and so on. I have felt as though I have been chasing my own tail. Getting straight answers to simple questions is difficult and sometimes impossible. When something goes wrong, memories suffer terrible dislocations; space and time don't correlate. All is blank. I am exaggerating, but not that much.

As for the Outremont Theatre, no one claims responsibility for the cost overruns and eventual suspension of the project. Obviously someone is to blame, but who? The entrepreneurs blame the municipal council, and it blames the entrepreneurs. The provincial and federal governments have, apparently, nothing at all to do with decision making in regard to this project, though it is difficult to believe that they would dish out $7.5 million without the slightest thought toward supervision. Yet this seems to have been the case. It is as though these top layers of government sought to avoid any and all responsibility for anything that might go wrong.

On April 20, 1999, *The Montreal Gazette* reported that the City of Outremont committed $11.5 million to the theatre renovations. Citizens claimed the total would be in the neighbourhood of $16 million after calculating legal costs, administration fees and the interest to be paid back on the loan over 20 years.[5]

During the three years that the provincial commission was investigating the cost overruns at the theatre, the lawsuit between the city and the companies hired to renovate the theatre was settled out of court, with the city agreeing to pay $1.2 million to the architects and engineers. The provincial commission was held up for nearly a year, delayed by court injunctions and legal wrangling.[6] When the 300-page report was complete, it was not released to the public. Outremont citizens, including former city councillor Céline Forget, who wanted to see the report were forced to request the document using the province's Access to Information laws. Even then the final report was not released in full, as certain passages had been withheld.[7]

Following his discoveries in Outremont, Philippe began to investigate the $24-million upgrade to the Jarry Park tennis stadium. Tennis Canada applied for infrastructure funding to improve the stadium and to build a number of indoor courts for the public's use.

PHILIPPE: *I travelled to Rockland Sport (an indoor tennis, squash and fitness centre) to meet with owner Peter Malouf. He was the vice president of the Quebec association of indoor tennis clubs, ACTIQ (L'Association des Clubs de Tennis Intérieur du Québec), in the early 1990s. At that time he spearheaded an initiative to explain to Tennis Canada and to the City of Montreal the reasons why costly changes and additions to the Jarry Park stadium were unacceptable and unnecessary. Malouf does not like the government. That much is clear. He thinks government houses and breeds incompetence, dishonesty and self-interest. It is not clear to me whether this is a preconception on his part, or whether he began to think this way as a result of his long struggle to stop the Jarry Park project.*

He said Montreal didn't need more indoor tennis courts, and listed some of the 16 centres that in 1994 offered a combined total of 189 indoor tennis courts in the area. He argued that an indoor facility without membership, like Jarry Park, can only hurt private facilities that have no choice but to charge membership fees to meet their operational costs.

PETER MALOUF: At Jarry Park they're competing directly against us in the private sector. We're the ones that have made a personal capital commitment to the industry. We're the ones who are really committed to the industry. I, as an owner, have invested in this club — to acquire this club, to renovate this club, to constantly upgrade the facilities. Where does it come from? It does not come from loans from the government, grants from the government. It comes from my pocket, ultimately. It comes from whatever profits are being generated from the club. I'm the one at risk. If things go bad, I'm the one that loses. If things go bad at Jarry, they spent $24 million of the public's money, and the people on the executive of Tennis Canada will not be affected by it.[8]

PHILIPPE: *Malouf's criticism of Jarry Park seems largely grounded on sound business sense. Jarry Park has an advantage at a time when indoor tennis courts are closing down because of dropping demand. But if the government, or Tennis Canada, expected to overcome the industry's malaise with the investment of public dollars, it was completely off track. Malouf doesn't believe that the Disneyland approach — build a beautiful stadium and invite some tennis stars to play there — will inspire lots of people to suddenly take up tennis. He feels that government programs encouraging tennis, and aimed at youth, would be much more effective.*

I took a ride to Jarry Park, where the Tennis Canada offices are conveniently located. I walked into the indoor facilities; the courts were dark and empty. The sliding doors of the sporting goods shop were half closed. I was told by the receptionist that there was no one there from Tennis Canada to answer my questions.

She told me that she would have someone call me. On my way out I turned back and asked her if the

park was always like this. "Mostly, in the summer,"
she said. I walked out. Every detail can become alarm-
ingly significant.

When Tennis Canada did call, a representative
informed me that all was well and that there was no
cause for concern. The money generated by tourna-
ments is distributed evenly to tennis programs across
the country. Unfortunately she did not have the time to
answer all my "petites demandes" because she was
extremely busy with preparations for an upcoming pro-
fessional tournament. She told me to expect a call back
in early September.

I received a call from the top man at Tennis Canada,
Richard Legendre. He is the director of Tennis
Canada, the director of the professional tournament
in Montreal and a former pro player. He informed
me that Tennis Canada has been in existence for 106
years and is responsible for the promotion and
development of tennis across the country. In the last
18 years the two major championships, one in
Montreal and the other at York University in
Toronto, have made $22 million in profits. Legendre
said the profits have been reinvested in the develop-
ment of the game, which boasts 3.5 million recre-
ational tennis players, 3,000 junior competitive
players and 4,000 coaches.

RICHARD LEGENDRE: Our project was well rounded and
ready. It was an important criterion back then. We had to be
able to start quickly, and there we were a step ahead of everybody else. We had been working on that project for the last
two to three years. So we were ready. We were ready to operate. We were given the green light and we got out of the starting blocks quickly, and that was important for the
infrastructure program.

There was a risk of losing our tournament status. Now
Montreal is on every tennis fan's lips around the world. It

is difficult to measure this impact but it is an important one. What really helped us with the project was the impact it had on things like tourism, international visibility and community service. It had a big impact on tourism, a major impact on Montreal's visibility around the world, which was part of our infrastructure argument to renovate the Jarry stadium.[9]

PHILIPPE: *But Peter Malouf had given me another point of view.*

PETER MALOUF: To hold a tennis tournament you did not need indoor courts. It was done outdoors. You did not need to spend $24 million for indoor courts. You could have fixed up a stadium very simply for an event that takes place for two weeks out of a whole year. I don't think the taxpayers needed to have their money blown away into a facility that was just absolutely unnecessary and redundant.

PHILIPPE: *The original application for infrastructure money was for $18 million, but didn't include the construction of indoor courts. Tennis Canada added $6 million and proposed building the courts to increase the appeal of the application. Legendre, obviously, defended the extra expenditure when he talked to me.*

RICHARD LEGENDRE: If the stadium only was to be redone, as was wished by the private clubs, we would not have survived. Politicians sensed this and said it would take a year-round facility at the cost of $24 million, which is better than an $18-million facility that would be used two weeks a year by the world elite. I think this decision was absolutely right.

There was a strong public dimension to the project in the accessibility aspect, maintaining a facility that is almost part of Montreal's heritage, maintaining Montreal's visibility. We were very confident about asking for public funds for this endeavour.

After two years of operation I can safely say that Montrealers are happy with the Jarry stadium and the tennis centre. I don't think we erred.

PHILIPPE: *Everything I have seen and read seems to imply that the politics of decision making starts with an idea springing forth at a precise moment and specific place. Then hands are shaken, projects are approved, pictures are taken of smiling men with nice clothes; black limousines slip away into the sunset and the idea is left to take its shape. But at what cost? And in whose interest? To me, the information and experience amassed these last weeks seem sufficient enough to make a very intelligent, critical statement about unaccountability, invisibility, confusion, misunderstanding, discrepancy, selfishness, greed and so on.*

We all know most people don't give a damn about government. Generation Xers, and to an even greater extent kids in their early 20s and younger, have no clue as to what's going on. We could argue that government and the media do everything in their power to stifle any interest that might surface regarding government. The government is always portrayed as being extremely dull and incomprehensible. We know that when you try to stick your nose in government business, there's no telling what you'll find, or if you'll find anything at all. Changing a country's attitude toward something as big, complex and inaccessible as government is a gargantuan task. Yet it presents, because of its obvious difficulty, a very compelling creative challenge.

I always thought that in the end I would get some politician, on his knees, to admit, "Yes, I did it! I'm guilty!" The weird thing is that at the beginning I didn't think I would get very far, but at the same time there was this tiny flame of optimism that maybe I could change something. Boy, was I wrong.

I feel completely useless. I think the project is a good one, but I don't think that I have the competence or the qualities necessary to pull through.

After seven weeks I have had enough; I'm not going to waste any more time and money. I can't take it. It's oppressing me. I am angst-ridden.

Quite frankly I think I would be more useful to this project if I were involved in its creative development. I don't have much enthusiasm left for research, but at the same time I do not want to dissociate myself from this project. I believe in it.

I think I could be more useful in another capacity, but I don't even want to speak to, or attempt to speak to, another politician. I put my toe in and the experience was debilitating, so I don't want to waste any more time or effort or energy.

When Philippe informed me that he felt he couldn't continue with his research, I asked him to reconsider and to write his frustrations out in a series of theatre sketches about his two months on the job, which we would later film for the documentary series. He accepted the challenge. Meanwhile Brigitte continued her work by researching the infrastructure funding to the Quebec City convention centre.

To be continued ...

NOTES

1. Infrastructure Works Office, Treasury Board Secretariat, Canada Infrastructure Works, Project Listing by Riding (Blue Books). List of all infrastructure projects approved as of March 4, 1997.
2. Lynn Moore, "Cirque du Soleil gets home in corner of Miron quarry: Permanent quarters will cost $30 million," *The Montreal Gazette*, June 21, 1995, p. A4.

3. Jeff Heinrich, "Intrawest picks up $10 million in government funds," *The Montreal Gazette*, June 29, 1994, pp. D1–D2.

4. Interview with Jacqueline Clermont-Lasnier was conducted in French and translated into English for use in this book.

5. Charlie Fidelman, "Outremont plows ahead with theatre plan," *The Montreal Gazette*, April 20, 1999, p. A7.

6. Charlie Fidelman, "Itching for a peek: Residents' lobby wants report made public on cost overruns for theatre renovations," *The Montreal Gazette*, August 3, 1999, p. A6.

7. Céline Forget [interview]. Interviewed by Jay Innes of Stornoway Productions, 2002.

8. Peter Malouf's interview in the fall of 1998 on the looming difficulties for private tennis court operators was an omen. In 2001, with rumours flying that Jarry Park was to receive more government handouts, Malouf sold Rockland Sport and it was transformed into a manufacturing plant. Another facility, Tennis St. Laurent, had already gone out of business.

   On June 3, 2002, the Quebec government (where former Tennis Canada director Richard Legendre is now minister of sport and tourism) joined with the City of Montreal and Tennis Canada to pay $12.8 million toward the expansion of Jarry Park. The construction of a 5,000-seat stadium and the addition of four indoor courts is scheduled for completion in 2004. (Pat Hickey, "Major upgrade for Canadian facilities: Tennis Canada will spend nearly $50 million to improve stadiums in Montreal and Toronto," *The Montreal Gazette*, August 10, 2002, p. H8.)

9. Interview with Richard Legendre was conducted in French and translated into English for use in this book.

CHAPTER 11

Alberta

When I was looking for a researcher in Alberta, one of the people we interviewed during the filming of *Days of Reckoning* suggested I get in touch with Lydia Miljan. Lydia, who lives and breathes politics, was completing her Ph.D. at the University of Calgary, studying the relationship between politics and the media. She is married with three young daughters.

> LYDIA: *It's been a pretty exciting week. I made a lot of calls and got lots back, even some I didn't place.*
> *Karen Kisser called from Western Economic Diversification (the federal government's regional development agency in charge of administering the program in the West). She parroted the line that "municipal governments made the decisions for what projects would be put through." She did volunteer the comment that in Alberta the program "worked well between the*

three levels of government. Money was given on a per capita basis. All three levels got along very well." I asked why all three levels got along so well and she wouldn't answer. She said it would be a question better answered by someone else.

She called back the next day. This time she had more information and she was now willing to tell me why the three levels of government got along so well in Alberta: (1) the municipalities were informed up front of the amount of money allocated to the community; (2) the federal and provincial governments provided criteria to guide the municipalities in selecting the projects — they knew the scope; (3) a democratic process was used at the local level; and (4) the city approved lists, and then went to the feds and provinces.

The standard line that is emerging from the federal government side is that, even though the feds may have reduced funding in general by off-loading responsibilities and cutting transfer payments in the last few years, the program was well liked by the municipalities even though there were tight time requirements for the completion of projects. Any decisions made were ultimately up to the municipalities. The underlying message is that even if the municipalities screwed up and gave money to marginal cases, the problem cannot be pinned on the federal government.

After all, we wouldn't want the government to "dictate."

Alberta was the only province to permit the municipalities a seat at the table where decisions were made, so we concluded that mayors and their representatives had far more say here than in the other provinces. But Lydia discovered that there were other players too. This became clear when she decided that she wanted to know what the rationale was for the decision to spend CIWP money on sports teams. At that point her investigation zeroed in on a $12-million renovation at the Saddledome (the home of Calgary's professional hockey team) which was funded under the infrastructure program. The province's other NHL team, in Edmonton, also benefited from the program, as did Alberta's two professional baseball teams.

This issue first came to the public's attention when the media reported that the Saddledome might receive CIWP money to build luxury boxes for the benefit of corporate clients. Art Eggleton, appearing before the Standing Committee on Government Operations, seemed to reject funding the arena, although he chose his words carefully, leaving himself some wiggle room at the end of his answer:

> We are not in the business of supporting professional sport or building luxury boxes or anything like that. If there are other aspects of that project that have to do with economic development, we'll have a good look at them.[1]

The counterargument from supporters of the Alberta sports projects focused on the public benefits resulting from this work. The prime minister picked up the theme while posing for pictures at a road-paving project in Alberta. When he was asked about funding for the Edmonton Oilers, he said that he didn't have a problem with subsidizing Edmonton's Northlands Coliseum because "the arena is used by people other than the hockey team."[2]

Ron Hayter headed the Federation of Canadian Municipalities during the push to establish the infrastructure program in the early 1990s. In an April 1994 article in the *Edmonton Journal*, Hayter was quite vocal in his belief that infrastructure money should be dedicated to roads and sewers and not used for upgrading arenas. The headline read, "Hayter cool to Coliseum proposal," and he was quoted as saying, "Now that the money is available, every group you can think of is trying to plug into it."[3] But that's not what he said when we talked to him in Calgary:

> I was critical, to begin with, of some of the projects that were proposed by the municipalities. I saw them as somewhat frivolous projects, and I wanted to make very clear the position of the FCM, that the bulk of the funding had to go for traditional infrastructure.
>
> The Coliseum isn't just a facility for hockey. It's a facility for the community. But if it's not upgraded — if it isn't an attractive

building — then it's going to create problems in attracting business to it. So in the case of Edmonton we looked at the fact that this was important to keep an important industry in Edmonton. It was not supporting the owner of the hockey team, as many people perceived, because the building would always be there, always owned by the City of Edmonton. In Calgary, I would assume, the same logic was applied.

LYDIA: *In Alberta the provincial Transportation Department was chosen to run the program, so an official face was put on the CIWP, as if it were all traditional infrastructure. They told me that everything is aboveboard, and I could get all documents through the city clerk's office.*

I walked down to the city clerk's office and took a look at the minutes from the meetings. They gave the official arguments of why we should have the Saddledome, why we shouldn't have something else. They're quite straightforward and they did have budget statements.

But my question is, how was it that the Saddledome ever got on the table? The minutes don't give me any idea of that. I wanted to know how one project got picked over another and I couldn't get the answer.

I went to the city, but nobody at the city wanted to tell me much. A city official said, "You should really talk to the people at the Saddledome Foundation. They're the ones who did the negotiations." So I went to the Saddledome Foundation. Nobody wanted to tell me anything. A representative for the foundation said that the decision was made by two people — one's retired, the second person is a hired consultant. I said, "Well, can I talk to the hired consultant?" The answer was, "No, no, we can't do that because he's paid by the hour and we don't want to foot the bill."

Then I asked for his name so I could call him myself. The answer: "Oh, we'll have to call him and see if he'd bill us." I've made several calls since, and I still am not any closer to finding out who this fellow is that bills by the hour.

So I called Robert Fraser, the manager of the Saddledome Foundation. He said he couldn't do much to help. He said it would be difficult to find anyone to answer my questions since this happened almost five years ago. While he is the manager, he said he must stay away from anything remotely political. I told him that I didn't accuse him of being involved in politics; I just wanted to know about the political process. He reiterated that he couldn't be involved. He then made the point of saying that didn't mean that there was anything to hide. He did volunteer, though, that had the Saddledome not received the CIWP funding, then the city would have been stuck with a rink without a professional team to play in it.

It's becoming very clear that the Saddledome was not initially high on the priority list for the city. In fact, it was not on the priority list at all. It only became a high priority when Calgary decided to keep the Flames in town and not pay for the improvements out of the city's coffers.

A review of some of the reports submitted to city council reveals that while Calgary owns the Saddledome, the city leased it to the Saddledome Foundation. In the original project report the Saddledome renovations and the Foothills Stadium (home of the Calgary Cannons baseball team) were not mentioned at all, or indeed placed on the priority list. What the city had to do to put the Saddledome on the list was drop three projects: the Bionutrient removal conversion, the Bonnybrook trunk rehabilitation and the Bonnybrook aeration system. These were ranked 37, 38 and 39, respectively, in the original report. Dropping the projects was rationalized by saying that water treatment could be funded by another budget.

When I asked for more information on the projects that were turned down, I was referred to Rick Smith, the alderman whose ward lost the Bonnybrook water treatment project. He said the Bonnybrook facility was considered a city utility and therefore the city would find another way to access other government funds by using a different budget. Although it was his ward that lost the treatment facility, he fought for the money for the Saddledome. Smith argued that the improvements to the arena helped keep the Flames in town.

RICK SMITH: We looked at the merits of having a professional sports franchise in our city and the economic value of that. It was determined that our major tenant, the Calgary Flames, was responsible for about $100 million per year of economic spinoff to the economy of the city; everything from Calgary Transit to restaurants and hotels, notwithstanding the fact that there are about 450 permanent and part-time jobs tied to the Saddledome. So with all those things in mind, we determined it to be a worthwhile project and worthy of funding.

LYDIA: *He said that the CIWP program coincided with the Flames needing to generate more revenue to pay for players' salaries. He said that they needed to build the luxury boxes, or "suites" as he called them, to get more revenues. The Calgary Flames have an important impact on the city because they provide 400 jobs or more, from concessions to management. With the infrastructure funding those long-term jobs were saved and a 20-year lease was put in place at a time when the city could have lost the team.*

In his mind the infrastructure project was gifted money. The only irritation was that the program caused the city to re-prioritize budgets already in place. Long-range plans were screwed up because they were funding projects that could be done in only two years. Less important projects were done because they could be done quickly.

Today I talked to one of the two people at Calgary's City Hall in charge of the CIWP: Tully Clifford in the Transportation Department. He indicated that he and a colleague, who has now retired, wrote all the project reports that were presented to city council.

The two men also were responsible for sending letters to the municipalities asking for proposals when the funding was announced. Tully was the first person to argue that the Saddledome was not all that controversial because the funding only went to public areas and the city owns the building. He was adamant that no public dollars went to private luxury boxes, as was widely reported in the media.

In a previous report I noted that the City of Calgary owns the Saddledome, but leased it to the Saddledome Foundation. By putting the Saddledome improvements on the list, the city would not have to pay the one-third municipal share of the project; the cost would be paid by the Saddledome Foundation. The Saddledome Foundation is an extension of the City of Calgary, with a mandate to oversee the management of the building, which was previously under a management agreement with the Calgary Exhibition and Stampede. The foundation had a surplus of dollars in its reserves that was earmarked for future renovations and improvements to the building.

All this is completely within the rationale and guidelines of the CIWP program. In fact, the federal government specified that it would look more favourably on projects with "creative" funding. In this way the city looked like the good guy, keeping its budget down and operating within the rules set out by the province and the federal government. This leads to the question, who is accountable to the taxpayers for the decision to put millions of dollars into the Saddledome?

Proponents of the decision say they were simply working under the rules set out by the federal gov-

*ernment and the province. The city didn't set the
rules. The city had to change its priorities to accommodate the federal government and it didn't want to
give up this "free" money. Officials in the federal
government were quick to point out that final decisions were made at the local level, saying, in essence,
that they were not responsible for the Saddledome
being funded, despite the fact that Ottawa put in
one-third of the funding. No one wanted to acknowledge that the taxpayer was footing a bill with no
effective representation.*

*Tully and I talked on the stairs at the Calgary
Centre for the Performing Arts while workmen were
running around renovating the lobby and washrooms
— paid for with $500,000 of infrastructure money.*

TULLY CLIFFORD: City council looked at the basic good
to the public when they considered the Saddledome project. They looked at things such as the concourse areas, the
restaurant and other areas that are accessible to the public. The initial application from the foundation said, "We
would like to do private boxes, we would like to do a
bunch of enhancements." What city council looked at
were the benefits from encouraging more events to come
into the city, and the spinoff economic benefits that these
events generate.

The council minutes don't capture all the discussion when
council is considering the infrastructure program projects. All
they capture is the bottom-line decision to take out the
Bonnybrook project and to put in the Saddledome.

Nowhere will you find a record of how the decisions were
made, why they were made, and the subsequent actions that
were taken by the city administration. In reality the only
people who know are the board of commissioners and myself,
as the manager of the program.

*More news on the Saddledome and the confusion over
exactly what was paid for with infrastructure money.*

The Saddledome Foundation was obligated in its lease agreement with the city to make improvements to the public areas.

When the city allowed the foundation to make the improvements using infrastructure money, it no longer had to pay the full share. It basically paid the city's one-third cost and did not have to pay the remaining $8 million. That $8 million was then extra money available to put into renovations in the non-public areas — those private boxes. So in a sense, even if everything is above-board in the accounting — and I have no reason to believe that it isn't — there's still the fact that a private organization got taxpayers' dollars to help subsidize something that it was obligated to do in the first place.

Jim Silye, the MP (Reform) for Calgary Centre at the time of the decision stood up and complained in the House of Commons as soon as the project was announced.

JIM SILYE: The Calgary city council last night, at a marathon meeting, agreed in a nine to six vote — this is at the municipal level — to use part of the infrastructure program of the government to renovate the Calgary Saddledome. For those members of the House who do not know what the Saddledome is, it is a hockey rink, a facility used in Calgary to house the Calgary Flames, the major tenants, and other programs and events throughout the year.... This is not the proper use of infrastructure funds. Only a few taxpayers will benefit at the expense of all taxpayers.[4]

LYDIA: *When I talked to Silye he made the point that it would be difficult to disentangle the money and the work because the private boxes and public areas were renovated at the same time. Bottom line, he said, the Saddledome did not have luxury accommodations before the Liberal's CIWP program.*

JIM SILYE: I saw a list of those projects that had been applied for under the infrastructure program in Calgary. I was looking for abuses. I did not see hockey rinks — I did not see any Olympic Saddledome on that list. It was only after it was approved that I found out about it.

Art Eggleton may have indicated in the House of Commons that MPs will be allowed to have input, but we had no input.[5] We had no say. I think if you were a powerful Cabinet minister and you were lobbying in your community, maybe you could get the money spent and participate that way. But I don't think too many members of Parliament did that.

I questioned the Saddledome because I felt this was subsidizing private business, and I objected to it. The answer came back, "Well, your mayor agreed to it and your premier agreed to it, and the rule is clear: if those two levels agree, then we don't object. So if you have a problem, take it up with them."

I have no criticism of the owners of the Calgary Flames for applying for the money, for negotiating the deal that they did, because I know that they are good, sound businesspeople whose intent is strictly to provide a first-class hockey team in this city. No question about that. And as businessmen, if the government wants to subsidize something, that's the first place you might as well look. It's easy money. It's quick money. It's not a debt and it's not a loan. You don't have to pay interest like at a bank. So if they want to give it to you, there's nothing wrong with applying for it.

LYDIA: *I don't know how the Saddledome got funded and it doesn't look like I'm going to find out. And I don't know if the folks at the Coliseum said, "If you're going to fund the Saddledome in Calgary, then you've got to fund the Edmonton Oilers" — because that door has been shut tight. I don't even know where the door is, quite frankly. I have no sense of the negotiation process between the governments and private organizations.*

There is a total lack of information about debate. I think those debates happened far away from any council chambers or management meetings. It makes me very skeptical because decisions were made where there were no records being kept. Certainly the people who

140

were around the table when they actually made the decisions are not making themselves available to answer any of my questions. I can't even find out who they are. Tully Clifford's comments, probably more than any others, at least helped me gain a perspective on the whole sorry process.

TULLY CLIFFORD: The national infrastructure program was not set up to intentionally exclude the public, but because of the timelines, there wasn't time to include the public, not even from a cursory point of view. When you have three levels of bureaucracy involved with any process that doesn't have a public component to it, there's a strong possibility of the public not being able to get full access to information. Whether there's a conscious effort to roll information under the carpet or not is subject to opinion. But I think, yes, there is that opportunity there.

The only public involvement was through the media. When the media was at council and said, "How can we accept something such as the Saddledome," or "Why wasn't this other project considered?" that was, in reality, the only access the public had. So in other words, no access.

The only way people could express any dissatisfaction would be writing a letter to their alderman or to the mayor or to council. All that would happen would be, "Thank you for your concerns."

It should have been turned into a public-hearing process. Members of the public would then have the opportunity to step forward, for example with the Saddledome, and say to council directly, "I do not see the benefit to me as a citizen. I see the benefit to the Calgary Flames and the people using it, but I don't see the benefit to me."

Under this existing infrastructure program, there is no requirement for a public audit. I think there should be a public-reporting component added to any subsequent programs so that the members of the public can see how the process works.

In Calgary, when you ask who is accountable, what I can say is, "I'm the manager of the program, and the projects were approved by council." Is that accountability? I'm not entirely convinced that it is. There's nobody who's clearly identified as the person responsible for the national infrastructure program, from a political or even, in lot of cases, from an administrative point of view. So there is nobody that you could point a finger at. That's a huge problem. We're accountable only to the program itself.[6]

LYDIA'S CONCLUSIONS: *I thought the job would be easier than it was. I thought that I could make a few phone calls and things would work out quite simply, that people would tell me the answers I wanted to hear, or at least give me an answer. It was a lot more frustrating than I thought it would be.*

It was difficult to be treated with such suspicion. I'd never encountered people being so suspicious of my motives. I've had to justify my existence and defend myself, when in fact I was asking them the questions. I'm getting so paranoid that I think there's a CSIS file on me because I dared to ask questions about the government.

The only problem is that the people who essentially helped a private enterprise organization get two-thirds of its costs paid forget that it was the taxpayer footing the bill. It's interesting that the people deciding to spend the money aren't accountable to their constituencies for the tax dollars they spend. No wonder the infrastructure program was liked by all the governments involved. No one is politically accountable!

One of the most telling statements I heard was by a former alderman who said that he did not want to embarrass the City of Calgary or the Saddledome or the Flames. All anybody seemed to be concerned about was not embarrassing these big hockey players, who can certainly take care of themselves and have lots of money behind them. Nobody wanted to embarrass City Hall, which has all sorts of veils of secrecy and doors that you can't get through.

I infer from this kind of reaction that the politicians and government officials are paranoid too. Either they're concerned that things are going to be taken out of context, which I guess happens, or they have something to hide — something happened behind closed doors that they're embarrassed about. And whenever people tell me that they don't want to embarrass somebody, I have to assume that there must be something to be embarrassed about.

You know, no one ever said that he or she didn't want to embarrass the Canadian taxpayers. That never came up. No one in this whole journey has ever mentioned that he or she didn't want to embarrass the taxpayers for voting for these guys who make decisions with no accountability.

NOTES

1. Canada, Parliament, House of Commons, *Minutes from Standing Committee on Government Operations* (March 16, 1994) pp. 23–24.
2. Brian Laghi, "Jobs the goal, not Pocklington — PM," *Edmonton Journal*, May 28, 1994, p. A3.
3. Mike Sadava, "Hayter cool to Coliseum proposal," *Edmonton Journal*, April 6, 1994, p. B1.
4. House of Commons, *Debates*, Vol. 133, no. 42 (March 22, 1994) p. 2595.
5. Art Eggleton commented on the MPs' role in recommending projects for CIWP in the House of Commons on January 21, 1994: "I know members of this House will take a close interest in the projects in their constituencies. For this reason we shall invite comments from each member of Parliament on projects recommended for his or her riding so that we can ensure that any information a member wishes to bring to our attention is available before a decision is taken." House of Commons, *Debates*, Vol. 133, no. 5 (January 21, 1994) p. 140.

6. In 2001 the threat of losing the Flames resulted in Calgary's city council granting more money toward the upkeep of the Saddledome. In a 9-5 vote council agreed to pay $3.9 million over three years. Rick Smith, former alderman turned chairman of the Saddledome Foundation, interpreted the decision as an indication that the "the city supports the team." (Canadian Press, "Calgary dishes out $3.9M to Flames to upkeep rink," *The Edmonton Journal*, June 26, 2001, p. A8.)

CHAPTER 12

Quebec Revisited

A THEATRE SKETCH FROM PHILIPPE: A man is sitting alone at a telephone, patiently dialling a number. He
has a Montreal telephone book on his lap, opened at the
centre section which contains all government contacts.

 The voices who will speak to him on the other end
of the line are amplified so the audience may share in
his experience.

 The telephone rings for a rather long time before
it is finally answered.

Voice #1	*Bonjour. City Hall.*
Man	*Hello, City Hall?*
Voice #1	*Yes.*
Man	*Hello, I was wondering if you could ...*
Voice #1	*I'll transfer you to someone who can. One moment please.*

Pause.

Man	*Hello, I am calling to find out who ...*
Voice #2	*One moment please, I'll transfer you.*

Pause.

Man	*Yes hello, could you please tell me ...*
Voice #3	*I'm sorry. There's no telling where you might find that information. Try Municipal Affairs. Have a nice day.*

He dials another number.

Man	*Hello, Municipal Affairs?*
Voice #4	*Yes?*
Man	*Yes hello, I was wondering ...*
Voice #4	*One moment please, I'll transfer you.*

Pause.

Voice #5	*Yes?*
Man	*Hello, I'm calling to ...*
Voice #5	*I'll transfer you, one moment please.*

Pause.

Man	*Hello, could you ...*
Voice #6	*This isn't the right department. Try the Executive Council. Have a nice day.*

He dials again.

Long pause.

Voice #7	*Hello, Executive Council.*
Man	*Oh, yes, hi, I ...*

| Voice #7 | *One moment please, I'll transfer you. Won't be too long.* |

A very long pause.

Voice #8	*Hello?*
Man	*Yes, I ...*
Voice #8	*I'm sorry. We don't deal with particulars. Try City Hall. Have a nice day!*

PHILIPPE: *Jay, thanks for suggesting I channel my frustration into the theatre and take my experience and translate it into some skits. It really interested me. I mean, instead of just being resigned and complacent and frustrated, I can communicate my experience in my own way, in my writing.*

What's really crazy is how much my experience resembles Kafka's novels, or the play I recently directed, Temptation *by Vaclav Havel. In the play the individual is confronted with this awesome machinery, impenetrable, obscure, mysterious, where there is no causality, where reason is compartmentalized. There are no links between one act and another and there's a lot of repetition — so much negative repetition. Those are the sort of themes Eastern Bloc writers excel at.*

I will not just be claiming that government is impenetrable. I can say so because I know! Thanks again. The experience has been invaluable to me.

BRIGITTE: *It doesn't seem as if there are any local municipal politicians who can tell me anything about the Quebec City convention centre. I will have to go for the big sharks.*

I went to the Ministry of Municipal Affairs in Quebec City and met the bureaucrat supposedly in charge. Before I asked him anything he had this I-know-nothing-this-is-not-my-job look on his face. At first he said he was in charge, but he later on changed his mind and gave me the name of another guy who is currently on vacation.

I wonder, though, what we could possibly find at the ministry. Its role is merely one of administration. When the municipalities sent their projects and the government made its decisions, the ministry was like a walkie-talkie between the two levels, or so a woman in the office of Laval's mayor has told me.

I spoke with Guy Vachon (the director of operations for the Société du Centre des congrès), who has been working on this project since the beginning. He told me that since there was consensus in Quebec City for the project, it was very easy for him and for everyone else to get support for the project from the federal government. And, as you probably know, Jean Pelletier, Prime Minister Chrétien's former chief of staff, is also the former mayor of Quebec City, so access was fairly easy, to say the least. Mr. Vachon said that they all agreed to a $27-million grant well before the CIWP was signed. It seems that the CIWP was simply the vehicle the feds had chosen to hand out the cheque. Quebec City was not part of the deal (not even through tax cuts). The total cost for the project was approximately $107 million ($27 million from the federal government and the rest from the province). Furthermore, the province is still paying for budget shortfalls and will probably foot the bill for a long time. Vachon agreed to be interviewed, but leaves today for a two-week vacation.

Here is a chronology I have assembled of the convention centre project:

May 1993 — Cabinet decides (decision 93-093) to draft the law creating la Société du Centre des congrès de Québec and to give the green light to the project, still under the condition of a $27-million federal contribution.

July 1, 1993 — The law is created. Administration members of la Société du Centre des congrès are to be named by the provincial government.

October 23, 1993 — Liberal majority is elected to the House of Commons.

December 22, 1993 — Art Eggleton confirms by letter that the federal government agrees to participate, under the condition of an agreement on the infrastructure program.

January 3, 1994 — Eggleton's letter is publicized in a news conference.

February 1994 — Canada–Quebec Infrastructure Works Program agreement is signed.

> *The decision about the construction site was nego-tiated between the provincial government, the munici-pality and the owner, who also owns the building next to the convention centre.*
>
> *The municipality handed out its assets in the for-mer convention centre for a symbolic dollar (the actual worth is $35 million, according to the mayor). The municipality was then able to collect property taxes.*

Earlier in my own research when I had talked to Claude Ryan, the Liberal Cabinet minister in charge of the program in Quebec when it began, he said that he was apprehensive about funding the Quebec City convention centre. But evidently close connections between the prime minister and Quebec City helped push the project forward. According to Ryan:

There was one project with reservations. And it was not our fault.

Quebec City had plans for a convention centre even before this program was developed and had approached the federal government. Since Chrétien's Cabinet director was the old mayor of Quebec City, there was a more or less implicit agreement, according to which Quebec City could rely on the infrastructure program for the centre.

Buried in the Canada–Quebec infrastructure agreement was the "fourth section" or "fourth envelope" clause that widened the infrastructure definition to include anything connected to "urban areas." The agreement stated that this fourth envelope was to be controlled by the province. This loosely defined definition, combined with a vague reference that the province would "consult" with the federal government, seemed to hand the province a blank cheque with no strings attached.[1]

BRIGITTE: *According to my spy at the auditor general's office, it is not likely that I will find such detailed records of the negotiations that take place when picking other spending projects. My spy says the important decisions are not written down. Only four or five ministers make the decisions, and those records are put in a top-secret drawer. Even the auditor general's office has a hard time getting this kind of detailed information. I get the point.*

I have come to the conclusion that Quebecers are bad managers but huge talkers. They are always ready to go on camera to say things like, "Look at what I've done! Am I great, or what?" So when it comes to projects like the Quebec City convention centre, they go on with remarks about how the region needed this facility, how every restaurant owner is happy, not to mention the hotels and various tourist-trap operators. Then, as a bonus, comes the now classic phrase: we have created X number of jobs! But when asked, "Yes, but at what cost?" or "What if, instead, we had put the money into daycare centres or into debt reduction?" they generally don't know, and appear pissed off to boot. Sometimes you may get the reply, "The theory that debt reduction creates more jobs than infrastructure spending has never been rigorously proven. We prefer to give our citizens something tangible for their money. With the help of the CIWP, Joe Citizen can come here and lounge about in our magnificent convention centre."

More political intrigue: I have discovered the reason for Quebec's delay in distributing projects. The government claimed the apparent inequities were caused by delays in handing out projects in Quebec, with its Bloc Québécois representation.

The delay was really caused by the change in power when the Parti Québécois defeated the governing Liberals in the 1994 provincial election.

The new infrastructure minister, Guy Chevrette, caused a storm when he announced that the PQ government planned to rescind all projects costing more than $1.5 million, claiming that the Liberals had used the projects to buy votes in the run-up to the election.[2]

In the end the new government called into question the validity of the decisions for a process that the federal government maintained was beyond reproach.

I spoke on the phone with Shirley Bishop, Guy Chevrette's political aide, about the commotion Mr. Chevrette created when he took office in 1994. She said that he thought there were too many projects, more than could be funded under the fourth section of the program ("great projects"), so he revised the list with the result that some projects had to be shifted to other sections. She does not recall any project that had been turned down by Mr. Chevrette and does not understand our interest in the so-called "Chevrette storm."

My contact in Gilles Vaillancourt's office, the mayor of Laval and the former head of the Union des municipalités du Québec, later confirmed that the PQ did not turn down many projects, at least nothing significant.

They revised everything (or said so) in order to be the ones who in the end accepted the projects and handed out the money.

That is pure demagoguery, but nobody seems to be complaining. Hey, it has worked this way for so many years ... why should we care?

I then spoke with Monique Gagnon-Tremblay, the Liberal Opposition leader and a former Treasury Board president who sat on the restricted committee overseeing the infrastructure program. She was quite stunned to hear that nobody I had spoken with seemed to think that Guy Chevrette had screwed up the program when he came into office. She said that, yes, he had made a mess, taking money from Liberal ridings and giving it to PQ ridings. She did not have the details at hand though.

I've just met with the president of the parliamentary commission on public administration, Liberal MNA Jacques Chagnon. He was the Quebec education minister during the first year of the infrastructure program. Chagnon said that when the Parti Québécois defeated the Liberals in 1994, the rules that limited funding only to new projects changed.

JACQUES CHAGNON: Soon after winning the election the PQ government had dictated new rules. They let municipalities integrate their infrastructure projects, as they themselves integrated government infrastructure projects, into the federal program, which really ended up substituting federal dollars in provincial or municipal projects. This was denounced by Quebec's auditor general, and with good reason.

BRIGITTE: *As the chairman of the provincial government's parliamentary commission on public administration, Chagnon asked the civil servants responsible for the infrastructure program to explain the reasons for the rule changes.*

JACQUES CHAGNON: We called in the deputy minister of municipal affairs, and he answered our questions. He was a little uneasy on the question as to why they had changed the standard. He said he did because he had orders to. It was obviously political, which everyone understood. You can't reproach a civil servant for following orders. He was just doing his job. He hadn't invented this new rule, the politicians had.

The political order could not have originated from anywhere other than the municipal affairs minister and the government that accepted it. It was in the minister's interest to please the municipalities, who could then include part of their existing capital budget in the federal infrastructure program. Municipalities would then have a third of their capital budget paid. Locally, everyone thought it was funny.

BRIGITTE'S CONCLUSIONS: *There are a few findings about the Quebec political scene that one may reach after three months' research of one particular program. One of those conclusions is that the political glitterati are closely related and, to my understanding, this is a little more obvious in the province of Quebec than in the rest of Canada. I don't know why though. Maybe the language, maybe the French culture, maybe the religious, historical or legal frame.*

It's harder to pierce the veil, if you will — to get secrets, to get behind the door.

One of the difficulties with finding commentators is that — and maybe this is too simple — they don't want to be bothered in their little lives. So I had the feeling that I was some sort of bug or mosquito and they were, maybe not afraid, but very uncomfortable talking to me. Because they don't know me; I am not from the known francophone media. They're a little afraid of being involved in some documentary looking at how the government works. They don't like the idea.

PHILIPPE'S CONCLUSIONS: *Now, I'm not a political theorist and I don't pretend to be. I didn't have a clue, when I started this project, as to how government worked. Five months later I still haven't any idea. There were a lot of secrets and a lot of closed doors. The government didn't want me to stick my nose into its business. It did just about everything it could to keep me at bay. I'm not a specialist. I'm not a journalist. I'm just an ordinary citizen. I have no place in government — I have no place even asking questions, it seems. At times I didn't even get to ask the question. Not only that, I didn't even get to the person to whom I wanted to ask the question.*

The distance that existed, or that exists, between the people that I tried to get in touch with and myself, that gap — I would like to share that experience with others.

Obviously the purpose of our project is not to intensify or accentuate apathy. On the contrary, the purpose is to get people interested in government processes. Because if a lot of people ask questions, then eventually the barriers will have to come down, and government will have to open itself up. I mean, that's almost a given to me now. Perhaps I'm dreaming when I say that. Perhaps I'm looking for utopia.

NOTES

1. The Canada–Quebec Infrastructure Program Agreement, February 7, 1994, p. 19.
2. Elizabeth Thompson, "Infrastructure projects on hold for evaluation," *The Montreal Gazette*, October 18, 1994, p. A7.

CHAPTER 13

Ontario Revisited

In Toronto Geoff Scales, who had just left a job with Via Rail, joined Deanne Corbett and Lori McLeod to tackle the big project in Ontario, the one that received the most money.

Ontario was the beneficiary of $2.8 billion in infrastructure spending that, according to Treasury Board, would create 33,000 jobs.[1]

In Phase I of the program Toronto dedicated most of the money to a project that the government boasted would create 2,280 construction jobs and generate another 4,000 jobs in the tourism and hospitality industry: the National Trade Centre. The team set its sights on this $180-million project.[2]

> GEOFF: *Each level of government I spoke to had a rationale as to why it became involved in this program. We were coming out of a recession and the federal government had an interest in creating jobs. (Ottawa was also interested in creating the photo opportunities, and*

thus political mileage.) The province got onboard because the gravy train was leaving the station. The municipalities gained because they were introducing projects that wouldn't have been introduced otherwise. While job creation had been a criterion at the provincial and federal level, it wasn't necessarily a criterion at the municipal level. That's what's problematic in a cost-sharing program: rationales change from the beginning to the end of a project because the rationale changes with the levels of implementation and involvement by each government.

The NTC project earned a lot of attention and a variety of comments. Toronto councillor Dennis Fotinos called it the "jewel" of the infrastructure program[3] while Mark Drake, the president of the Canadian Exporters' Association, said, "This is part of the boondoggle going on under the so-called infrastructure program ... at taxpayers' expense."[4]

The idea for a convention complex that would include a trade centre had been thrown around since 1987, when it became clear that the professional sports teams were leaving Toronto's Exhibition grounds and people feared for the survival of the historic buildings and the area. City council tried entering into a public-private partnership and developed the plans for a new convention centre, attached to an office complex. Projected costs were $450 million. The plan was based on the assumption that $360 million would be split evenly among the municipality (Metro Toronto), the province and the federal government, leaving $100 million to be raised by the private sector.[5] Soon after the 1988 election was called, the Tories stated publicly that the federal government was not going to take part in the project.

With the federal government out of the funding equation, the private sector took a pass on the project, and a smaller plan for a trade centre was conceived. The new plan called for a 750,000-square-foot extension to a renovated building, at a cost of $180 million.[6]

During the election campaign in 1993 the National Trade Centre became a political issue when angry unemployed construction workers confronted Prime Minister Kim Campbell during a campaign

156

stop outside a radio station in Toronto and demanded that the centre go ahead.[7] Jean Chrétien's Liberals vowed to support the Trade Centre, as they had done with the Quebec City convention centre, so in effect the project was guaranteed even before the terms of the federal-provincial agreements were negotiated or the management committees struck.

GEOFF: *When the CIWP came along the federal government walked in with a bag of money and plopped it on the table, and the wheels started spinning at the Metro level.*

The rationale of Metro was that it was free money, and there were a number of interests involved — construction, job creation and so forth. Metro councillors had other options before them. But it was felt that the NTC would open up new business possibilities for Toronto and that Metro had to be competitive with other North American cities. As the province was paying one-third, the federal government one-third and Metro one-third, the case was made that there was all the more reason for each level of government to pursue something like a trade centre, which may not have gone through under normal circumstances. Hence, the cost of building the centre was reduced from a government's jurisdictional point of view, though not from a taxpayer's point of view.

DEANNE: *I started the day at Metro Hall. Blake Kinahan was one of the three councillors who opposed the NTC. He didn't remember that fact at first, so I had to show him a newspaper clipping to remind him. Apparently there was a report commissioned by a consulting company that identified several concerns about the NTC's ability to generate profit. This fact, however, didn't deter council from pushing the project through. Kinahan said that he opposed it because he tends to be conservative when it comes to spending public money and likes to make sure that due diligence is taken when approving a project.*

No one I've talked to so far has had anything commendable to say about our representatives' duty to make sober, unbiased decisions. Even when a cost-benefit analysis is done and a potential problem is identified, no one pays any heed! It's incredible.

GEOFF: *I talked to Ruth Grier, who sat at the NDP provincial Cabinet table as environment minister during those days when the NTC project was approved. She was able to offer the municipal politician's perspective, as she had served for 15 years in local government before moving to Queen's Park.*

RUTH GRIER: We developed a formula and told the municipalities late in 1993, early 1994, "Here's the pot of money that will be available to you. You submit projects that would qualify for that funding. If you can't spend it all, tell us, and we will reallocate to other municipalities or to boards of education" — which also had a pot of money. But once the municipalities had submitted their projects, we didn't get into the nitty-gritty of saying, "That's a good project; that's a bad project." We let them make those decisions.

There was no project-by-project analysis of projects that municipalities put on the infrastructure list. I don't know at what point the city put the National Trade Centre on that list, but once they decided that it would be on that list, we would not have second-guessed it. The debate and discussion about whether to build a trade centre would have occurred before the decision to put it on the list.

I don't know how much the existence of the infrastructure program accelerated the decision to put the Trade Centre up front and to get on with it. I suspect that, as in many other major projects, it was a factor in the timelines, but I think the decision to do the Trade Centre was certainly made at the city and the Metro level.

The council vote for the Trade Centre was 30 to three in favour of the project. One of the councillors who joined Blake Kinahan in opposition was Ila Bossons. She said she felt pressure from several directions to approve the Trade Centre proposal, which would commit a majority of Toronto's infrastructure funds to a single project:

I did not support that decision. I didn't think it was worth the risk. I was not convinced that the business plan would really justify spending $180 million on that one particular building. Toronto wants to be on the map, on the North American map, and the National Trade Centre was a glory project. The word "national" should give you a hint just how obsessed this city was with getting a piece of the glory. My concern was that every major city on this continent is building a trade centre.

There are two ingredients in many decisions a councillor makes. One is facts. The other is pride. There are probably some councillors who didn't even read the reports, who only made their decisions based on the pride factor. Political decisions are not physics or mathematics, where one thing has to follow logically upon the other. There are emotions involved in decision making. So the facts don't always count. The more glorious the project is, the less the facts will be considered. That's the reality of decision making. I suspect that's true from the smallest village council up to Ottawa. Now, you can say this creates tens of thousands of man-years of work, but it is tax money. For the next 20 years, is this project going to drain money from those same people, in the form of taxes to maintain it?

One of the factors in the decision was that the centre would get an exemption from provincial taxes. That would of course help to make the business plan look wonderful. Other trade centres — for example, the International Centre, which happens to be not in Toronto but near the airport, in Mississauga — do not have the privilege of not paying taxes. It is a rather unfair way for one city to promote its trade centre over a trade centre that may be competing with it. But I'm sure that persuaded a few more people at Metro council to vote for it.

There was also political pressure from the trade unions and the construction companies who wanted us to create jobs. That project was built when the economy was pretty slow. We had a conference table full of people in hard hats, occasionally shouting opponents down. They wanted those jobs. I didn't feel the pressure of the unions, but obviously others did.

Canadians pretend that they have a modern, up-to-date country. In reality it isn't. All you have to do is look at which cities have good sewage treatment. That's sort of the basis of civilization — what you do when you flush. It goes back to the Romans. Montreal only a few years ago stopped flushing directly into the St. Lawrence River. Victoria still dumps all its sewage into the ocean. We are a long way from cleaning up that part of our environment. There are many small towns that desperately need help with having better sewage treatment. We've got cities that don't have a safe water supply. That's Third World.

Toronto city councillor Jack Layton was vocal in his opposition to government-funded megaprojects like the SkyDome. But Layton, who is a high-profile member of the Federation of Canadian Municipalities, admitted that he reversed his stance on supporting megaprojects when it came to the NTC:

The rationale of the program changed, to some degree, from the original Federation of Canadian Municipalities concept, and the definition of what constituted infrastructure became broader. In big Ontario cities, for example, the sewage treatment was already up to reasonably good standards, so people began to look at other interesting kinds of economic development projects. The National Trade Centre certainly wasn't the kind of thing that the FCM had initially been talking about, not at all.

You've got to have roads and sewers, but you also have to have facilities for economic development purposes. The National Trade Centre was a good example of using the infrastructure program to produce spinoff benefits. There's ongoing investment in the city as a result of the Trade Centre. It produces a sort of shadow or echo effect through the years.

In the case of the National Trade Centre there seemed to be a broad consensus, across a broad range of groups who normally don't come together. People like myself and social groups who normally oppose megaprojects like the SkyDome and railway land development and things like that came together. We saw it as potentially creating jobs for working people, regular jobs as opposed to the high-flier sorts of jobs. It had that sort of mystique about it. If it doesn't turn out that it accomplished that, that'll be quite sad.

The Trade Centre is a piece of urban infrastructure. It is part of what allows a city to thrive. To me it's like investing in a university or investing in a port or investing in an airport. Over the long term it could be a real economic engine for Toronto. It can make us a centre for idea exchanges, which is what the great cities of the world are. They never are manufacturing centres for very long.

LORI: *We spoke with Gail Bernstein from the International Centre in Mississauga. Gail gave us some important distinctions between trade and convention centres, and told us that, while the NTC is a great building, it could never deliver on its promise to bring international business because trade centres don't do that, convention centres do.*

She said trade centres are regional, and if people are coming to town for shows they usually fly, meaning the trade centre doesn't have to be in a city, it has to be close to an airport. This means the argument about being right in the city isn't valid, she said, since people have work to get done at trade shows and don't usually come for a holiday like they do at conventions: "People in my industry certainly looked at the figures and understood that there would never be enough operating income and that there would have to be a government subsidy to get the building built and to keep that building operating."

She appeared before the public hearings on the Trade Centre to express her concerns. She said she went

*in good faith as an industry professional but her com-
ments were dismissed.*

GAIL BERNSTEIN: We hired a consultant to help us to communicate with government. Like many consultants, he was
an ex-bureaucrat and an ex–elected politician from a highly
regarded political consulting firm. He knew the process, and
he was advising us on how we should present our point of
view. We said to him, "We want to tell the government that
they can and should build this project because that property
is old and run down and needs to be revitalized. But we've
done some analysis and we think it could be done for
$50 million."

Our consultant said, "Please, don't make a fool out of
yourself. Don't even say that to the politicians. If you're going
to say that, don't even refer to a figure less than $100 million.
They'll laugh you out of the room because a project of any less
scope isn't even worth talking about." His experience was "big-
ger is better."

The committee allowed us to speak to them, but I don't
think they listened. I think they dismissed what we had to say
as being of no consequence, as being biased, and as being fear-
ful that our business would be negatively affected by the
National Trade Centre. Anything we had to say was rejected
out of hand. As the general manager of the International
Centre, I really was offended by that. We are experts in the field
that they were endeavouring to get involved in, but they dismissed what we had to say as "sour grapes."

That project could have been done, the building refur-
bished, for $50 million. Even if we're wrong and it was $75 million, it would have been more than enough for the business
that it's really doing, which is local business or business that
they already had. It still would have acted as a catalyst for new
business. But it would not have been a burden on the taxpayer,
with an operating deficit which no one talks about, but is going
to continue for all eternity with that building.

The public should be mad. I don't know if they'll ever find
out, and if they do, who are they going to blame? There's no

accountability. There's no identifiable prime mover behind any of this to come back to and say, "That was a dumb thing, why did you do it and what are you going to do now to make up for doing it?" At least, there isn't anyone that I've been able to find.

> LORI: *Private business doesn't build in a vacuum ("Hey, let's spend the bucks now and figure out if it will work later") but this seems to be the party line on any questionable projects ("Oh, don't bug us yet, it's too early to tell if we can justify building this megalithic structure with your money!").*
>
> *Since my previous job was as a stock market reporter, I find that I keep looking at the government as I would a public company, with myself as a shareholder (albeit very, very minority). If you look at things in this frame of reference, the lack of accountability in the spending process and the devil-may-care attitude is frankly a little annoying. At shareholders' meetings people get pissed if the store they've invested in doesn't sell the kind of underwear they like or they think the restaurant's coffee sucks (both true stories from past annual meetings I attended). Maybe I'll stop paying my taxes and do a little private investing instead.*

CONCLUSIONS FROM DEANNE, LORI AND GEOFF: *We headed down to the CNE grounds this morning for a site check and to talk with Joe Pantalone, a city councillor, chairman of the board of governors of Exhibition Place and the former chairman of the National Trade Centre building. He was also an active member of an organization called the Toronto Job Start Coalition. The coalition was made up of government and private sector representatives, including the construction industry and the labour movement, and it lobbied the federal and provincial governments to invest, in order to get the economy moving in Toronto.*

163

JOE PANTALONE: Toronto had the road-building under control. We had our recreational centres and arenas under control. We've been investing in that for many years. We had our transit system sort of under control. We're not dumping raw sewage into the lake, like some other cities. We're not like Montreal or some other places. People in Toronto pay taxes like everybody else. We were intelligent and forward-looking in our planning.

It became feasible to fund the National Trade Centre under the infrastructure program ... the federal government could appear that they were nice to Toronto. People across the country think that this is some rich province, even though we have more poor people here within defined poverty limits than some provinces have residents. It probably would not have been politically sustainable for them to say, "Here, Toronto, here's $60 million." They're always building museums worth hundreds of millions of dollars in Montreal or Quebec City, but somehow the country is unified in hating Toronto, so you can't give anything to Toronto. And they didn't give anything to Toronto. All they did is give us our share because they were giving something to everybody.

At the time the provincial government wasn't sure whether they should consent to the National Trade Centre under this Infrastructure Works Program. The municipality said, "Hey, the program is supposed to work on the basis that we suggest the projects. It's not top-down, it's bottom-up." The whole community was convinced that we needed something like that. Mr. Art Eggleton and Mr. Jean Chrétien during that election said that, if they were elected, they would fund the building of the National Trade Centre in Toronto.

We were arguing also that the centre was needed because the tourism industry — which has been a pillar of strength in Toronto, with something like 21 million visits a year to the city — was suffering. Within that general context the Trade Centre was deemed by everybody to be one of those pieces of economic infrastructure that was essential if this city were to compete on a world-regional basis.

DEANNE, LORI AND GEOFF: *But Gail Bernstein had told us that the success of trade shows is decided by the surrounding population and Toronto's distance from the large American markets would be a problem.*

GAIL BERNSTEIN: Just because we built a building doesn't mean they're going to come. Politicians and bureaucrats don't understand that there's a regional aspect to trade shows. For example, the shows that run in the Chicago trading centre are there primarily because the trading market within a 500-mile radius of Chicago is, I believe, 70 million people. If you were running a show in Chicago and you were going to have 30,000 attendees walk by your booth, versus running that same show in Toronto and having 3,000 attendees walk by your booth, which show are you going to go to?

DEANNE, LORI AND GEOFF: *The public was never told, and hence never really understood, the true costs of the NTC. They were told that it would cost $180 million and that the city was only paying one-third of that, $60 million, through the CIWP. They probably understood that it was one of the more expensive projects under the CIWP. What wasn't shouted from the top of the CN Tower was the fact that the NTC was being financed through debentures. But Joe Pantalone didn't seem very worried that the money had been borrowed.*

JOE PANTALONE: When you factor in the debenture and the interest on that debenture, the true cost to Toronto for the Trade Centre is higher than $180 million, of course. Listen, when you buy a house and you buy it for $150,000, by the time you finish paying for it, it probably cost you $300,000. Does that mean you don't buy the house? That's not how our decisions are made.

Let's not blow it out of proportion. It is not really that much money. I mean, the program was extended to five years, eventually. If you divide the $2-billion federal contribution over five years, for the whole country, it's $400 million a year. That's less than building the SkyDome.

DEANNE, LORI AND GEOFF: *The last word on the subject goes to Jack Layton.*

JACK LAYTON: The National Trade Centre is showing close to a $9-million shortfall every year. We had long discussions about this at council, and a lot of tough questions were asked. But what do you do about a situation where you have a large facility that's losing money? What do you do, close it? Everybody resigns and says, "We made a mistake, we'd better all quit and let somebody else run the city"?

The National Trade Centre was supported on the basis that it would bring Toronto the high profile and stature it deserved while delivering much-needed jobs. But the big bonus was that it offered the prime movers and shakers of the project the opportunity to be recognized for delivering on an idea born in the mid-1980s. This fascination with visibility, credit taking and photo ops seems to have been one of the prime motivations for making CIWP funding decisions — not surprising, I guess, considering that at any one time there were at least three times as many politicians vying for the spotlight than is usual!

NOTES

1. *Renewal Agreement for Tripartite Infrastructure Works Program Signed with Ontario* [media release]. Treasury Board Secretariat of Canada, May 2, 1997.
2. Royson James, "Trade Centre a sure thing, sources say," *The Toronto Star*, July 31, 1994, p. A6.
3. Fotinos was quoted in Royson James, "Trade Centre approved by 30-3 vote," *The Toronto Star*, May 10, 1994, page A6.

4. Drake was quoted in Jonathan Ferguson, "Exporters call trade complex big waste," *The Toronto Star*, August 11, 1994, pp. C1, C8.

5. These figures were quoted by Joe Pantalone when he spoke to Geoff in the fall of 1998. Pantalone was chairman of the committee that oversaw the construction of the National Trade Centre on behalf of the then Metro Toronto council.

6. Royson James, "Trade Centre approved by 30-3 vote," *The Toronto Star*, March 10, 1994, p. A6.

7. Kim Lunman, "Jobs issue dominates campaign: Liberals promise $6 billion public works," *Calgary Herald*, September 11, 1993, p. A8.

PART III

In Search of the Powers That Be

"I think that you should go talk to the powers that be."

Susan Thompson, mayor of Winnipeg,
responding to the question "Is there anyone specific you suggest we
talk to find out how the infrastructure decisions are made?" during an
interview in the fall of 1998.

CHAPTER 14

Signs of the Times

As Anette had discovered in Manitoba, politicians were extremely interested when it came to getting to play the infrastructure Santa Claus and taking credit for high-profile projects. Stories about ribbon cuttings and other photo ops exploded onto the pages of every daily and weekly newspaper in the country, and the red-and-white signs that Charlie Campbell talked about were not confined to Prince Edward Island, but dotted the landscape from the Avalon Peninsula to the Queen Charlotte Islands. The Cirque du Soleil wasn't the only infrastructure circus!

> ANETTE: *Today I spoke with Bill Comaskey, mayor of the City of Thompson. He is one angry mayor. He says he isn't happy with the federal and provincial governments and is eager to tell his story. Comaskey is an excellent conversationalist with many colourful anecdotes.*
>
> *He said Thompson wasn't treated fairly in the infrastructure program. He told me his northern*

Manitoba town applied for $3.4 million in infrastruc-
ture funding to repair collapsing sewer and water lines
in the Burntwood trailer court. He held off the work as
long as he could while waiting to hear that the project
had been accepted. Eventually work was started, even
before the project had been approved. When the take-it-
or-leave-it decision came back from Ottawa, he was told
that the federal government and the province would
only pay $860,000 each and Thompson would have to
pay the remaining $1.68 million.

To top it off, he said, the other two levels of govern-
ment wanted all the credit.

BILL COMASKEY: Once the project proceeded, we received a sign. The sign was quite colourful. It had the Government of Canada, the minister responsible on one side of it, and on the other side it had the minister responsible for the provincial government. In the middle it was blank. Any mention of the City of Thompson was left out.

The Government of Canada wanted to take most of the credit for it, and the Government of Manitoba wasn't far behind. We were told that we had to put the sign up, we were told where it had to go, and we had no say in the matter whatsoever. Even the cost of erecting the sign was ours — we had to pay the labour cost to have the sign installed!

We weren't doing the project because we wanted credit for it. All we asked for was fairness, and we don't believe that we did get fairness in the overall project. It was just frustrating for us that the other levels of government would take full credit for the program when in fact they were not paying their full share.

Many of the projects that were funded were, in my view, grandiose projects. I don't believe the Saddledome in Calgary and many projects across the country that were in the arts and entertainment sector should have qualified for the infrastructure program.

Even in Manitoba they had a project in Assiniboine Park that certainly did not, in my view, qualify for this basic Infrastructure Works Program.

172

So I wish that the Government of Canada would have accepted the rules as presented to them by the Federation of Canadian Municipalities and not tried to use the program for political gain.

> ANETTE: *The mayor told me that when the project came close to completion, Thompson received a brass plaque to be mounted at the ribbon-cutting ceremony; the plaque only named the federal and provincial ministers, not the municipality. The mayor said, "If we're not included, we're not going to put this up." Eventually the Infrastructure Secretariat made an exception and added the municipality's name to the plaque and the ceremony proceeded.*

> BRIGITTE: *The signs! Usually the permanent signs here are in brass, about two feet by two feet, and are located near the entrance of the convention centre, theatre or whatever building it was that received funding. And usually space on the signs is divided equally between the feds and the provinces. The exterior signs, on the construction sites, are much bigger of course (approximately six feet by four feet). They're white with black inscriptions. On the signs there is a phrase saying that the project is made possible by the participation of both governments, under the infrastructure program. Both levels of government have the same importance. Only sometimes does the municipality have its name and logo, in a different colour.*

In Ottawa an Access to Information request turned up a detailed media analysis that revealed the government's concern over the public perception of the program. The 900-page analysis was composed of weekly graphs and summaries of all the media coverage of the program — from the smallest radio station in northern Cape Breton to the largest TV broadcasters in Toronto. Articles from the country's newspapers were sorted by positive or negative public reactions to themes like job creation and claims of harmonious federal-provincial relations.

ANETTE: *I am intrigued by this fascination with political visibility. The more I search, the more I realize that it plays an enormous role in politics. It seems to make or break friendships and deals.*

It felt pretty good to talk to a fellow who had done some research on the infrastructure signs in 1994 after construction on the projects had started. He told me how he drove home one day after work and noticed a big infrastructure sign and he wanted to know more.

He said he had seen similar signs at the Winnipeg Art Gallery that seemed to be there for months prior to the start of construction. Another infrastructure sign was erected 25 feet up at a busy intersection, far away from the actual construction site.

He wondered how much all these signs cost and how many there were in Manitoba and across the country. Who makes them? Are there specific measurements and colours for each sign?

He called the federal government's regional development agency in charge of the program to ask whether it reuses the signs or just throws them away. How many signs are out there? What's the bureaucracy's role in erecting the signs?

People he talked to told him they would get back to him and never did. Some of them even became annoyed with him. After four weeks he said he couldn't get an answer to any of these simple questions so he gave up. I told him I know eight other people across Canada who feel the same way!

All he could conclude from the search was that the government seemed to be more concerned with advertising the job than the job itself.

I asked him if he would appear in our documentary to tell his story. He refused, flat out. After a little bit of prying he told me that he is a government employee and he's worried what would happen if people at work found out.

The minutes from the Ontario management committee meeting on September 11, 1997, indicate that 12 officials — from Industry Canada, the Treasury Board, the Ontario Ministry of Transportation, the Ministry of Municipal Affairs and a representative from the municipalities — had spent a considerable amount of time negotiating the order in which federal and provincial politicians would be called and notified of an impending ribbon-cutting ceremony. The minutes give no indication of any discussion or debate on projects that cost millions of dollars.

Former Ontario NDP Cabinet minister Ruth Grier said the different levels of government worked together smoothly, as long as everyone followed the rules:

> The province assumed the responsibility of making sure that the applications were legitimate and the figures added up, and as the money flowed there was some oversight as to how it was being spent. The federal government didn't wish to exercise any of that control.
>
> The only slight hiccup came when some of my colleagues got over-enthusiastic and announced projects as soon as they were approved, without asking the federal member of Parliament to be there for the photo opportunity. I think there was a kerfuffle about that. At that point the federal government certainly made it plain to us that while they didn't want to nickel-and-dime us, their members had to be there to have their picture taken at the same time. It's entirely legitimate that both levels of government wanted to get the credit for what was going on. I certainly never turn down an opportunity to be on camera.

JENNIFER: *I have spoken with someone who is sure to be of interest. Jack MacAndrew is a well-known Prince Edward Island personality who was hired by the*

*Atlantic Canada Opportunities Agency to ensure all
the infrastructure signs were up and prominently dis-
played around the island so people knew who to thank
for the work.*

*Jack has worked for the both the provincial Tories
and the Liberals. He's full of opinion — much of it
knowledgeable — and openly said that he thinks the
whole infrastructure program is just a way for politicians to get re-elected.*

JACK MACANDREW: Let me tell you something. In my experience it's real easy to make sense as long as you're not spending
your own money. So as long as governments can dip their
hands into the public purse and use the public's money to
aggrandize themselves as a political party, well, it's easy to do.

Over the past winter we were called by the federal government, through ACOA, to put up about 50 signs across Prince
Edward Island. Now, my function in this was essentially to
arrange a little bidding thing with three or four of the people
who make signs and to administer the program and make sure
the signs got put up on time. So the sign company put up these
signs, all over Prince Edward Island, saying that this is a joint
federal-provincial project. Clearly the federal government is
very interested in taking as much credit as it can.

Now, these were signs that were either four-by-eight plywood, erected with pieces of four-by-four wood driven into
the ground, or the signs were smaller, about two feet by three
feet. They were very simple, really. They just said, "A joint
project of the federal government and the provincial government," and described the project.

Red and white were the colours of the signs we erected. I
believe that red and white in combination has been known to
appear on signs ordered by the Liberal Party of Canada for
election campaigns. I really don't know whether it would be
coincidental or not. I didn't ask, quite frankly. I was told to
make them a specific shade of red and white.

They spent about $17,000 to $18,000 on signage across
P.E.I., as I recall. That was the total bill. The signs were supposed

to go up last November and they didn't go up until this April, when the frost finally went out of the ground, because they just couldn't get their act together. So the project went on about six months longer than it was supposed to go on. There was no payment made to anybody until the signs actually went up.

Hundreds of thousands of dollars were spent on signs all across the country. Hundreds of thousands of dollars! I could never, fundamentally, see the reason for all these signs in the first place — except pure, crass credit taking, which amounts to vote buying. I participated in that process because they called me to do it and I had the standing offer. Somebody had to do it, so I did it. But, really, the thought of spending money on these dumb signs which litter the countryside. I mean, if you can't do better than that as a government to have people think you're doing a good job, I really don't see that signs around the countryside are going to achieve the desired effect.

And it never occurred to them that somewhere, somehow, someday, these signs are going to have to come down. It certainly was not part of the original contract. Perhaps the people in the local community, once the signs get battered enough, will take them down because they're unsightly. I see some of the signs when I drive around, and look at the lovely red-and-white colours, but to me they're just part of the landscape.

> JENNIFER: *Jack wasn't the only person I talked to with strong opinions about the visibility and the value of PR. When I did my interview with Tom McMillan, the former Mulroney Cabinet minister from the island, he was candid on the subject.*

TOM MCMILLAN: It's great for the politicians. As a member of Parliament myself, I loved to be photographed with the local mayor, with the local members of the legislature, with the local businesspeople. It was good politics to be associated with a good news story. But with the advantage of hindsight, now that I'm out of politics looking back, I can see that a lot of those things of which I was so proud at the time were a great cost to the taxpayers.

I was always aware that a program like the Infrastructure Works Program in 1993 was a highly attractive boondoggle. Politicians love to cut ribbons. They love to have big four-by-eight plywood signs extolling the virtues associated with them through roads and sewers and bridges. The federal government by definition is heavily involved in areas where it's very difficult for federal politicians to get credit. There's not much political credit at the ballot box for foreign aid, for national defence, for research and development, for bilingualism.

Excuse the pun, but roads, bridges, sewers, wastewater treatment plants are concrete; people can see them. They drive on them, they go by them, and they can certainly see a great big four-by-eight red-and-white sign that says, "This is our gift to you, courtesy of the federal government and the local member of Parliament." If he's a Cabinet minister or she's a Cabinet minister to boot, all the better. They've been extremely skillful at marketing the infrastructure program as a benefit to the taxpayer.

Politically speaking, it's a gift that keeps on giving. If you go into any constituency in this country, chances are you will see a big plywood sign advertising that this — whatever "this" is — is the gift of the federal government. In many cases that sign has been up since the 1993 election, even though the relevant project may have long since been finished. It is excellent politics. It is superb marketing. It is wonderful electioneering because it's geared to the next election. But it is certainly not good public policy.

> ANOTHER SKETCH FROM PHILIPPE: A man walks into a government office and approaches the secretary sitting at a desk. She looks up and smiles.

> Man   *I am looking for the decision maker.*
> Secretary *That's him over there. But he can't be bothered at the moment. He's behind closed doors.*
> Man   *I have a little bit of time. I can wait if that's all right.*

Secretary   *Oh, you can wait all you want, but he seldom comes out from behind those doors.*

Man   *Can I wait here?*

Secretary   *Please do. But like I said, he seldom comes out from behind those doors.*

Man   *I understand.*

Secretary   *Very good. Some people take forever to understand that. It almost seems like they purposely resist understanding. Do you understand? Hahahaha.*

Pause.

Man   *May I ask you what he is doing in there?*

Secretary   *I see you coming. You're not the first, you know. Don't think he's avoiding you. He'd more than gladly meet with you if he knew you were here. But even I seldom get to speak with him directly. He's very, very busy.*

Man   *If I left a message for him, would he return it?*

Secretary   *Messages are like dead weight to him. He favours human contact, a firm handshake, a solid yet friendly tap on the back, that sort of thing. Do you understand?*

Man   *I understand.*

Secretary   *Very Good! You understand also that he is nothing like you and me. He's one of a kind.*

Man   *Hmm.*

Pause.

Man   *Maybe you can help me.*

Secretary   *Really! Please, how?*

Man   *I would like to know in whose interest he ...*

Secretary   *Well, yours of course. What a silly question.*

Man   *Then why is it I ...*

Secretary   *Things take time. Of course you know the saying: great things come to those who wait.*

> *Look at him. If you wait long enough ... but like I said, he seldom comes out from behind closed doors.*
>
> Man   *I understand that.*
> Secretary   *Very good!*

The next day.

> Secretary   *You again. I didn't think we'd see you here so soon. Thought we had gotten rid of you for good. Hahahaha. Official humour, you understand.*
> Man   *Is he still behind closed doors?*
> Secretary   *You just missed him. He's gone ribbon cutting.*

And at every sod-turning or ribbon-cutting ceremony, at every artificially created event designed to bring the media into the presence of politicians standing in front of a handful of beaming staffers and hangers-on, the point was always emphasized in clear and ringing tones, by the MPs, MLAs or city councillors, that with the infrastructure program the governments had delivered on their promises to create jobs.

CHAPTER 15

Have I Got a Job for You?

So what came first — infrastructure or jobs?

The answer to this question seemed to depend on who you talked to. In the House of Commons Art Eggleton, president of the Treasury Board, claimed:

> The program will have a substantive impact on unemployment ... the Federation of Canadian Municipalities has estimated that for every billion dollars invested, some 20,000 jobs are created.... The infrastructure program is an integral part of the vision of the new Liberal government to lay the foundation for economic recovery, to kick-start a sluggish economy and provide a future for Canadians.[1]

However, Eggleton's successor as Treasury Board president, Marcel Massé, placed more importance on the job factor; in the April 12, 1997, edition of the *Ottawa Citizen* Massé was quoted as saying,

"The purpose of the infrastructure program is to create jobs in the short term."[2]

Indeed, when our researchers posed the "Which came first?" question to people in their respective provinces, the responses varied, depending on the person's expertise and his or her role in the infrastructure program.

Former Ontario Cabinet minister Ruth Grier said that Bob Rae's NDP government saw job creation as the top priority:

We found ourselves in the worst recession since the Depression, and Ontario and the Maritimes were particularly badly hit. The rationale was clearly jobs. That was what the people of Ontario desperately needed, and our government saw it as an opportunity to get some federal money at a time when the federal government was beginning to retrench with respect to spending.

On the other hand, in Manitoba Juergen Hartmann, manager of employment, training and education for the City of Winnipeg, said that for his municipality creating jobs was secondary to infrastructure: "In the infrastructure process the need for the work was established beforehand. Of course, it was serendipitous that we were in an economic crisis in terms of labour supply and labour demand, and it just happened to be a fit."

M. Saeed Mirza, who conducted an intensive study of the infrastructure program and presented his findings in a 1996 McGill report on Canada's infrastructure, drew a different conclusion:

The infrastructure program was basically designed to create jobs. If the federal government, along, of course, with the provincial governments, were genuinely concerned about the state of infrastructure in Canada, they would not have conceived such a program over such a short period. [Like] other issues in our society — health, education and social security — infrastructure is an issue which doesn't just stop after a period of five or six years. Infrastructure has to be maintained continuously.

Guy Breton, auditor general of Quebec, concurred with Mirza's analysis:

> If from the beginning the word "infrastructure" had been the key word, we would have been much more strict about the definition. But in my mind the key words were "job creation" because we had to generate economic activity. The excuse was infrastructure, and luckily it needed work. The government came running to save the infrastructure because it had fallen into such disrepair, but in my mind the government's purpose was not saving infrastructure but handing out work and money to people. But it could have been shipbuilding, for all it mattered.[3]

In the early stages of my investigation when I was looking for someone to guide me through the intricacies of the collective government mind, I was referred to a former deputy minister who had recently retired from the public service. I went to meet him in a mutually agreed-upon location, a burger shop, and he was easy to spot — seated at a corner table with his back to the wall, the collar of his jacket turned up and the brim of his tweed cap pulled down. I felt like I had set up a meeting with Deep Throat during the height of Watergate. He talked in a low, conspiratorial voice while his eyes constantly scanned the room. I thought, "This is a perfect example of Ottawa paranoia." He pleaded ignorance to most of my questions before he refused my request.

But as he was leaving he passed on some sage advice that I should have taken to heart. He got up from the table and whispered, "You're crazy. This is their baby! Jobs, jobs, jobs is the core. This goes a long way back. You're getting yourself into a real maze."

In the big blue binders I had received from Treasury Board there was a column listing the number of jobs created by each project. During my infamous meeting with the Treasury Board officials I asked how the government had counted these jobs. I was told flatly that a job-creation formula was used to estimate the numbers. I couldn't see the formula because it was the property of Statistics Canada. I was simply expected to believe the numbers that the federal government offered up for public consumption in the House of Commons, such as those cited by Art Eggleton on December 15, 1994:

> ... as we reach the first anniversary of the launching of the program when the prime minister and the premiers came together on December 21 in Ottawa, I am pleased to be able to bring some good news to the members of the House. At the halfway mark of the program over 80 percent of the $6 billion has been allocated to some 8,400 projects, creating over 81,000 jobs for Canadians. We are well on the way to the creation of the 100,000 direct jobs in the program.[4]

I asked Treasury Board to respond in writing to my request to examine the job-creation formula. Several days later a fax arrived with an excerpt from a letter to a person or persons unknown, written by the information commissioner. In this letter the commissioner ruled in favour of the government's decision not to divulge the formula:

> During the course of the investigation discussions were held with officials of both the Treasury Board and Statistics Canada in order to determine the availability of the information to the public and the conditions under which the Treasury Board received the input/output model simulations from Statistics Canada. We found out that the production of the input/output model simulations is one of the products and services offered by Statistics Canada on a cost-recovery basis. The service is available to the general public and is not restricted in any way. The cost for national and interprovincial models is apparently in the $600 to $700 range.
>
> In this case the product created by Statistics Canada for Treasury Board was custom tailored to particular parameters and specifications requested by Treasury Board. And it has been confirmed that the input/output tables were based on short-term job statistics collected by Statistics Canada by various means. The data within the model simulations is neither updated nor maintained by Treasury Board Secretariat. The final product was sold to Treasury Board for $39,600 (Statistics Canada's cost to produce the simulations) under an end-user

licensing agreement which permitted the Treasury Board to use the product while it remained the property of Statistics Canada. This agreement is "non-exclusive, non-assignable and non-transferable" and does not allow the Treasury Board to "sell, rent, lease, lend, sub-license or transfer the data product" to anyone else.[5]

Smooth. I was not permitted to see the formulas because the Access to Information Act does not apply to material that is available for purchase by the public.

The ruling from the information commissioner indicated that Treasury Board had provided the "particular parameters and specifications" to permit Statistics Canada to custom tailor the product. I filed an Access request seeking the information communicated by Treasury Board to Statistics Canada before the formula was created, along with the final report from Statistics Canada. My thinking was that I could compare the inputs and the outputs to get some idea of the formula that linked the two.

The request for the final report was flatly turned down, while the input information I received was limited to a letter dated March 22, 1994, written by George Anderson of Treasury Board to Statistics Canada's assistant chief statistician in charge of national accounts and analytical field studies. In the letter Anderson referred to a personal meeting with people from Statistics Canada in which they had the opportunity to meet and discuss the nature of the input/output models.

Simulations (models, formulas or whatever the word of the day is) were required for the following categories: roads, highways and airport runways; gas and oil facilities; dams, irrigation and electric power construction; miscellaneous infrastructure projects (including marine construction, waterworks and sewage systems and other engineering construction); non-residential construction; and repair construction. Mr. Anderson wrote, "In all, 66 simulations will be required at a cost of $700 each, but some of the models could be run together to reduce the cost."

While much of the letter left me in a fog, and still does, I was able to take from it another example of the tight time constraints and the pressure for visibility present in the program. In Anderson's letter he indicated that there was pressure on Statistics Canada to develop the formulas quickly because ministers would be making project announcements the following week. As a result, he asked that some of the 66 simulations be ready the next day and the remainder be completed within three days.[6]

Rather than allow them to intimidate me, I sent another Access request, this time asking for the actual number of jobs created by each project. I also asked for an explanation as to how the government knew the numbers of jobs indicated in the reports were accurate.

The response to this request came in the form of yet another letter written by George Anderson, addressed to the assistant deputy ministers representing the federal regional development agencies in charge of administering the program in the provinces. In this letter Mr. Anderson mentions that the job-creation estimates sent in by the municipalities in the first days of the program were not consistent and a "standard approach for reporting jobs" was required. This would "avoid the problem ... of poor data from some municipalities, of inconsistent methodologies and also of ignoring important off-site employment associated with supplying infrastructure construction and repair." The letter also updated the decision to have Statistics Canada produce simulations that would include both "direct on-site and off-site jobs."[7]

I became really confused. But stick with me and I'll try and spell it out.

The intent of the formulas, said the letter, was to generate a table that would provide the numbers of jobs created per million dollars spent by a province for various types of infrastructure work. For the whole country about 15 jobs per $1 million would result, which would produce 85,000 direct jobs for the $6-billion program. Mr. Anderson said it was recognized that in some cases the estimates would overstate or understate "what is known about direct job creation for the project," but said this "highly reputable estimate of general spending effects will save the need to develop expensive and time-consuming data collection on a project-by-project basis" and is as sound an approach as any possible within a reasonable cost.[8]

So that's the way job creation was calculated! It hardly seemed worthwhile to rush Statistics Canada into creating 60-odd models in three days, when it was already determined that 15 jobs would be created for every $1 million spent across the country.

Also, in Mr. Anderson's letter the assistant deputy ministers were told that the preferred way to communicate the job-creation announcements would be that "project X will create N direct jobs both on-site and off-site." N would be the number for the jobs created across the country for that particular project.

The use of the letter N may have been intended to indicate jobs created in the country as a whole, but what it really told me was that I was following the trail of a very smart bunch of public servants who would avoid using words that were too specific and could paint them or their political masters into a corner if someone like me wanted to count the actual number of jobs created by a single project in one particular province. These guys were crafting statements that were so general they couldn't be accused of misleading the public when making job-creation claims.

The final bit of information revealed in Mr. Anderson's letter was that they didn't want to state the number of jobs created in any single province, although he feared "some provinces will push for this."[9]

George Anderson's name and phone number appeared at the top of another document I received through my Access request — something called a "House Card," dated April 26, 1994. It was one page, labelled "Infrastructure Program," and it appeared to contain a pre-set question to be asked by someone during Question Period in the House of Commons: "My constituents are looking forward to having jobs through the Canada Infrastructure Works Program. I wonder if the minister can tell us with more precision how many jobs Canadians can expect to have generated by the program and when these jobs will become available?"

Under the heading "Suggested Response" were six points that could be used to answer the question. Included was a statement that "pre-designing and engineering jobs are under way, tenders are being called and 196 projects worth $306 million have been approved in Nova Scotia, Manitoba and Saskatchewan." The information indicated that 5,247 construction jobs were "expected to start soon" and that "it is estimated that 90,000 jobs will be created by the program." The definition of "on-site" and "off-site" was followed by the recognition that the number of jobs in each community "will vary depending on the mix of projects applied for and the population of the area." Under the heading "Background" was the reminder that prior to the start of the program it was estimated that 60,000 jobs would be created.[10]

I did some more digging and discovered that during Question Period on April 27, 1994, all parties had stayed close to this script that was written only one day earlier. For example, the Liberal MP for Trinity–Spadina, Tony Ianno, directed these comments to Art Eggleton:

> My question is for the minister responsible for infrastructure. As the government moves forward with the renewal of Canada's environmental, communications and transportation infrastructure, many of my constituents in Trinity–Spadina are looking forward to the new jobs that will be created by the program for today's and tomorrow's economy.
>
> Can the minister tell us how many jobs Canadians can expect to have generated by this program and its spinoffs, and when will these badly needed projects commence?

Eggleton responded:

> Mr. Speaker, I thank the honourable member for the question which gives me the opportunity to give more good news to this House on how this Liberal government is getting Canadians back to work.
>
> Since I reported last Friday we have had an increase of $8 million of projects that have been approved, another 400 people, and we are now up to 5,500 jobs. We have approved over 350 applications and we have another 1,000 in the pipeline. What is more, there are people in rural Saskatchewan at this very moment constructing and reconstructing roads for the benefit of the citizens in those communities.
>
> Finally, the original estimate of 60,000 jobs has now been revised as a result of accurate data from Statistics Canada.[11]

Later, when I requested an updated list of infrastructure projects, I was told that the out-of-date summary would have to suffice. Access to Information co-ordinator Donald Rennie informed me Treasury Board was not going to update the master summaries because that would mean it would have to design a program to make the information "machine readable" (whatever that means): "The office of infrastructure does not regularly produce a document of the actual number of jobs by projects for Phases I and II. The reports are not machine readable. In other words, a program must be designed to generate this information."[12]

Finally, I was informed that "there is no documentation that specifically answers your question asking how the government knows the number of jobs created is accurate."[13]

Because Statistics Canada sells its services to the public, it would create formulas for me if I paid $40,000 and provided the necessary input information; but Treasury Board would not allow me to access the input information that was shared with Statistics Canada to develop the 60 models. I had no way of replicating the inputs to re-create the formula. All I could hope to do was to find some smart statistician, make an educated guess at the inputs, pay Statistics Canada $40,000 to develop the formula for me and wait to see if the jobs totals per province matched those published by Treasury Board!

I gave up on my search for the Statistics Canada formulas.

By now we were well into summer and the researchers were busy tracking down elusive politicians and running into problems of their own in the search for job-creation answers.

Lydia's political science savvy, coupled with her Western straightforwardness and confidence, made an instant impact when she called the Treasury Board's communications department. Brian Biggar obviously didn't connect her with me.

> LYDIA: *Brian Biggar returned my call. Oh mama, is this guy a live fish or what! I had the most unbelievable conversation with him. It took over an hour for him to tell me absolutely nothing.*
> *Permit me to expound.*
> *Before I could ask too many questions he quizzed me, asked about the project and myself. I gave him the standard response, said I was a summer student, blah, blah, blah.*
> *On the question of how they calculated the number of jobs, he started by saying that we couldn't get the methodology because Statistics Canada held a "patent" on the formula. When I asked him how a government*

department could patent anything, he said that Statistics Canada is a Crown corporation, and like any Crown corporation, it acts independently and "at arm's length" from government. He reiterated — I don't know how many times because my eyes began to glaze over — that Statistics Canada is not a government department. He then proceeded to explain that, like any Crown corporation, it was allowed to have trade secrets: "After all, you wouldn't expect CBC or CN to provide information to its competitors, would you?"

As for the "technical questions" that I kept asking him, he referred me to Randy Poon, who is the "resident expert" at the Treasury Board and who should be able to answer the questions.

At one point in this exchange I asked him, "Who's accountable for the CIWP?" His response was, "Ask your master, Preston." Alarm bells went blaring. I, in my most indignant, self-righteous voice, said, "I beg your pardon, what did you just say to me?" He was so clueless he couldn't even recall what he had said and responded, "What do you mean?" I replied, "You just said for me to 'Ask my master, Preston.' What is that supposed to mean?" He said that he didn't mean it the way it sounded, but then asked, "Don't you work for the Reform Party?"

I replied that I had no idea where he might have got that information or impression; I certainly did not introduce myself with any political connections. He said, "Isn't Stornoway Preston Manning's residence?" I corrected him by saying that Stornoway is the residence of the leader of the official Opposition and that the film production company name had nothing to do with politics. He apologized and thanked me for clarifying the company's role and my affiliation.

He said that Statistics Canada is the premier statistical outfit in the country and that its numbers were to be believed. If it said 11,000 jobs were created in Alberta, then I should believe it and not be so cynical. I told him that if I tried that line in my Ph.D. defence, I would be laughed out of the room. Besides, I informed him, I had worked with Statistics Canada's numbers in the past and they were not infallible, despite his endorsement. He dismissed these comments as my being overly cynical about Statistics Canada.

I then asked him what effect the CIWP had on the jobless rate in Alberta. He said, "You do the math: 129,000 jobs have been created from start to finish in Canada. Find out the jobless rate and figure it out." I asked how I could figure it out when he wouldn't give me the real body count. He said that they couldn't attach bodies to those figures because some of those jobs may have been part time, so, for instance, there might have been 15,000 people hired under the CIWP. I said that there might also have been only 6,000. He said that couldn't happen. I said sure, one person might have been given two part-time jobs. He conceded that might be possible.

I started to have fun with this guy since he was in such a mood to talk. I asked him how, if I couldn't get numbers on the actual people who worked or the jobless rate, could an average citizen measure the success of the CIWP. He said that 11,000 jobs were created in Alberta, and the government spent $676 million. Wouldn't that indicate success? I said, "OK, let's divide 11,000 jobs into $676 million to see how much each job ..." Interrupting me he said, "You can't divide those numbers. Do you realize how much a bridge costs in material to build?"

I asked how the populace could judge the merits of the federal government's job strategy program? He said that the program created 11,000 jobs in Alberta. Wasn't that a measure of success? And around the circle we went again. I asked him whom I should I talk to about these decisions. He said that I should call the Prime Minister's Office and ask PMO officials to defend the merits of the job-creation program.

Biggar was also especially keen on my asking questions at the grassroots level since that's where the decisions were being made. When I told him that every level points its finger at the other levels, he said that I shouldn't accept that kind of response. Each should be accountable.

Great advice!

The next time I talk to him I'll ask how the government could tell if all these jobs were really new jobs or simply jobs that weren't lost.

When I took Brian's advice and spoke to Randy Poon, he said the numbers emerging from the formula were only an estimate and admitted that there was no way of comparing the estimate against the actual number of jobs created because it would have been extremely expensive.

Reports from other frustrated researchers who were tracking jobs began to roll in. Anette was attempting to find out what impact Manitoba's Infrastructure Renewal Demonstration Program was having in that province. It was the only program in the country that purposely hired people who were collecting social assistance.

ANETTE: *I tried to get specific numbers on jobs created and on the whole job-creation business. I went to Social Services in Winnipeg. I was referred from there to the Infrastructure Secretariat, which referred me to the City of Winnipeg Public Works Department, which again referred me to Social Services, all on the same question. And I still don't have an answer on just simple job-creation figures.*

I had a conversation with an official at Public Works. I asked if there were any numbers on jobs created or any estimates. He said, "No, we don't have any numbers." I said, "Why don't you have any numbers?" He didn't know the answer to that, he just said,

"We don't need any numbers, we know the program was successful."

I said, "How do you measure the success of a program without any stats and numbers?" He said, "Because we allocated money to the needed infrastructure — and I feel very good about how we allocated funds because we gave disadvantaged people work." I asked what he meant by "disadvantaged people." He said, "People without skills." I asked if these people were taught new skills on the job or if they had been given training before the start of the job. He said, "I do not know."

I then spoke with Juergen Hartmann, manager of employment, training and education for the City of Winnipeg, and he offered his opinion on the job program.

JUERGEN HARTMANN: Infrastructure Works could be described as a short-term fix. In the absence of any suitable fix, a short-term fix is better than no fix at all. It makes sense in terms of providing unemployed people with work, which in the end provides long-term benefits to the community at large.

In other words, if you rebuild a section of road or a section of water mains, that may be in place for 80 to 100 years. You ought to find opportunities where the expenditure that you make on unemployment insurance and social assistance is complementary to a need like infrastructure renewal, and that's what we did in Winnipeg.

JENNIFER: *I don't think I was very successful at all in finding out how many actual jobs got created because of the program. All I was able to find out was that a project went ahead and that there was construction work for five or six weeks in the summer.*

As the P.E.I. auditor general pointed out in his recent report, nobody went back to see how many jobs were really created: "There is no indication that the employment levels indicated on project applications

*had any bearing on those projects selected for funding.
As well, there was nothing to suggest that the employment levels were reviewed to ensure that they were
reasonable.*"[14]

We consulted other audits done by the auditor general of Canada,
the provincial auditors of Nova Scotia and Saskatchewan, along with
one done by a private company for the Government of Ontario.

In the federal auditor general's 1996 examination of the program,
entitled "Lessons Learned," he reported that the government's job-
creation figures may have been off by as much as 35 percent, calling into
question the Treasury Board claims that the two phases of the program
would create 100,000 short-term jobs and 10,000 long-term jobs. The
criticism was based on the belief that 35 percent of all projects would
have gone ahead regardless of whether they received infrastructure
funding, so they could not be counted as new jobs created as a result of
program spending.[15]

I know that when I first heard the government state that tens of
thousands of jobs would be created by the program, I assumed that those
were long-term jobs for people in need of work. But the auditor general
also reported that the federal program files showed little or no monitoring information to indicate the actual results, and he criticized the general terms used to describe the success of the job-creation program:

> We believe the limitations of the estimates ought to be pointed
> out in reporting them to the public and to Parliament. This was
> not always done. For example, the 1996–1997 Estimates Part III
> of the Treasury Board Secretariat notes that "total program
> expenditures by the three levels of government ... will have cre-
> ated about 74,000 jobs during the first two years...." The basis
> for this number was not explained, and no allowance was made
> for any possible shortfall in the program's additional invest-
> ment effects. Our analysis of additional investment effects sug-
> gests that the real levels of additional employment created
> directly by the program were likely lower than those announced
> by government.[16]

The provincial audits also found fault with the ways in which the job-creation component was handled. The Ontario audit reported that the provincial government failed to set any minimum standards for job-creation objectives. The auditor general of Nova Scotia said that the employment-creation outcomes were not reported in the program's accountability documents because the estimates were the sole source of information on job totals.

> LYDIA: *I can't believe it — nobody went out and counted heads. No one said, "Let's look at the books of the private contractors and ask them how many people were hired?"*
>
> *I went to one of the job sites and I asked the superintendent, "How many people did you hire?" He said, "We hired between eight and 13 people for the job."*

Professor Richard Soberman, chair of civil engineering at the University of Toronto, was commissioned by the federal government to provide an outside assessment of the infrastructure program. His 1996 report commented positively when it concluded that the federal government got almost all of its $2 billion back through the collection of income taxes, GST and the reduction of social assistance payments to people hired to work on projects. The report went on to say that the only way the federal government could justify intruding into provincial jurisdiction was with the promise to create short-term jobs and that it "is by no means clear that this particular shared-funding initiative should become a permanent federal government program."[17]

The Soberman Report determined that the infrastructure program cost $60,000 per job created; however, the report noted that the same money could have created long-term benefits for the country's youth, had it been invested in daycare centres. Had funding been diverted to pay down part of the national debt, the report claimed, the investment would have had the same impact on the economy as CIWP.[18]

Professor Soberman had assembled a panel of experts to comment on the infrastructure program and these comments were included at the end of the second of the report's two volumes. For some reason there was no attribution for any of the statements. David Gillen, an economics professor at Waterloo's Wilfrid Laurier University, sat on Soberman's expert panel. He told me that he felt the report was used by the government to give the appearance of accountability and to serve as a "rubber stamp" of approval just prior to the announcement of the $1.3-billion extension of the program.

One section of the report assessed CIWP's effect on economic growth. The assessment was done using national and regional econometric models, designed by Informetrica, a private competitor of Statistics Canada.

Professor Soberman had requested the econometric models from Informetrica to double-check the work done by Statistics Canada. The information on the assessments was contained in the second volume of the report.

I couldn't make sense of it.

I sent the volumes to McGill University economist Reuven Brenner, an expert in this area who sometimes works as an advisor to government. When the word "economist" is mentioned to Professor Brenner, he doesn't try to hide his disdain, comparing most present-day economists to the astrological advisors who in years gone by advised kings and emperors on policy. He agreed to read the two volumes of the Soberman Report and comment on the formulas. After he'd examined the contents of the report he wrote me a letter outlining his conclusions:

Dear Jay,

I skimmed over the two volumes of the Soberman Report. I doubt if anyone has ever read these two volumes, certainly not the second one. You know what this is? It's the full employment act for economists and consultants. As you might have noticed, in the summarizing document they refer all the time to the supporting documents. But in fact there is nothing in the supporting documents to support the numbers in the main document! Where are the econometric studies?

Briefly: lots of abstract generalities, a lot of randomly summarized mishmash, but there is absolutely no way to double-check what all these consultants have been doing! Neither the database, nor selection of data, nor the econometric tests, nothing, nothing, they are not there. Typical.

Informetrica refers to TIM and RIM.[19] Here's what they are saying: "TIM is a sophisticated simultaneous model with extensive current-period and dynamic linkages between and within each segment of the model structure. TIM incorporates a 112-sector input/output model to consistently represent the simultaneous relationships between detailed final demand categories and the 112 industry output measures." Now to the end the paragraph: "The unique level of detail allows a more straightforward introduction and evaluation of judgmental and other non-model information such as product-specific information from Canadian Capital Projects, an inventory of major investment plans maintained by Informetrica Limited."

And what does this sentence mean? "RIM is based on a top-down articulation of regional economic measures, both provincial and territorial, based on national forecasts from TIM."

Well, it's absolutely meaningless. First they are talking as if Canada had 112 very well-defined sectors. Well, if you think about our economy today, when the borders between industries are blurred, telephone and Internet and postal services, and Internet and entertainment and games and telephone services, well, what are those 112 sectors that are so well defined? I don't have a clue and they don't provide it.

Then, to take themselves off the hook of such criticism, they say at the end, and this is what you said you don't understand, "the unique level of detail allows a more straightforward introduction and evaluation of judgmental and other non-model information." In other words, to escape this, whatever they defined as the model, if it doesn't come out the way they wanted, they can introduce a judgment. Now, what is that subjective judgment that they introduced? It's part of that secret that you mentioned, and because it's the property of somebody, you cannot have access to their judgment. So what does it mean? Nothing, zero, nil, that's what it means. Jargon and pseudoscience.

And who bothers to read this report? It's a perfect recipe. I think it's much better than Valium, actually. No decent economist has been using these types of large, Keynesian models — that is, this TIM or RIM — for years.

As I said, I am sure nobody — nobody — ever read this.

Regards,
Reuven

JENNIFER: *I have met with Andy Wells, a former provincial deputy minister of the Treasury Board who has retired. He said the federal government only introduced the infrastructure program to look good at a time when it was cutting back everywhere else. He said to be wary of the way job totals are expressed.*

ANDY WELLS: Look at the methodology used to arrive at the number of jobs this program created. If they're looking at person-hours, for example, and then somehow or other translate that into jobs, that's a very questionable method of arriving at a useful answer. If you look at how many permanent jobs were established and track those jobs, I think you'd find a very different kind of answer than what we're hearing.

The job creation in this province [P.E.I.], if you were able to look carefully at the various jobs, you'll find that they were EI or UI directed. In many cases this was a way for the province and the federal government — but more the province — to get people the necessary weeks of work so that they would qualify for unemployment insurance. That was an important objective of the program for local politicians.

This is a game that the provinces, and particularly the Maritime provinces, have played for years. The reason they do it is because UI is not out of their pockets. The alternative in many cases is welfare, which is out of the province's pocket. So the information that you get from any analysis of this kind of program, I would say, is very suspect.

JENNIFER: *But when I met with Leo Walsh, he saw the job-creation controversy a little differently.*

LEO WALSH: When you look at government responses to acute situations, whether it be regionally, nationally or even in the international forum, we often rush in for short-term goals. They may be expensive and inefficient, but maybe in the end they are worth it because there is an acute need. This was viewed as "something should be done now," which changes the atmosphere or the environment in which decisions get made. And that's not necessarily bad.

There is nothing better than people getting up in the morning and going to work. Nothing makes people happier. This program made that kind of a short-term economic impact. It created jobs for people. That means paycheques at the end of the week, which is the best test of development. It might have been expensive, as some might suggest, but it achieved its objective of short-term stimulus to the economy and it created a lot of optimism.

BRIGITTE: *OK, I have read the Quebec auditor general's report. As you will notice, it's quite hard to fully under-stand the various elements that were supposed to be taken into account in the management of the infrastruc-ture program. Mr. Breton (the auditor general) could not, however, tell us more in his interview than is already in his report. Not because he did not want to be more spe-cific, but basically because the law forbids him to do so.*

He did slip in this pointed comment about his early days as an auditor.

GUY BRETON: When the Union Nationale took over from the Liberals at the end of the 1960s, my work involved travelling through rural areas. When the Liberals were in power there had been mechanical mowers on tractors that cut the grass along the side of the roads. In the months following the Union Nationale's victory, I began to see workmen with scythes cut-ting the grass along the roads.

199

On the one hand the grass was cut and jobs were created; but on the other hand we had gone back in time at least five or six years before the Liberals' decision. Jobs can be created if you ask people to do menial jobs, but is this the best way to use public funds? You also have to be efficient. Of course the opposite is also true. If you use machinery to such an extent that you don't need people, the investors make money but there are fewer salaries and less taxable income. You need a balance between the two extremes.

I finally escaped from my adventures in job creation by going to see Professor Brenner in Montreal. He thinks the government's job-creation strategy is misguided:

All that we want, and all Canadians want, is to prosper. So the question is, are these jobs creating wealth or not? And I would say the whole focus on job creation is wrong; governments can always create jobs.

If you look at communist countries, they never had any unemployment. How did they do it? Well, everybody had to go to work. If you didn't work, you were defined as a hooligan and you entered into the criminal statistics or you were in jail and not counted at all. Governments can also enlist people in the army and the unemployment rate will go down.

There are other ways in which the governments can create employment. If they make a country very poor they might not, let's say, import snow-removal equipment, and then the people have to shovel or clean snow with teaspoons. You will have plenty of employment but you will also have a lot of poverty.

The issue is what types of jobs the country is creating — not just whether someone is employed or not.

I can issue a decree tomorrow that everybody who is unemployed no longer gets unemployment benefits but gets a government salary instead, that's it. Presto, you have 100 percent employment and no unemployment rate at all.

What shall I do with those people? Well, does it matter? Of course it matters. I can ask them, "Please show up and clean the streets every morning at five o'clock." Will they contribute something? Maybe.

I can also ask them to please just show up and dig a hole in the ground. Would that be productive? Really, we are just playing with words here. That's exactly the point: you can always play with words, and governments are very good at that.

There is another problem with this whole issue of job creation by governments. They are saying, "We are spending $8.3 billion on this program." Let's say this money created some jobs, forgetting the quality of the jobs. What is not evident, what is never taken into account, is how many jobs were lost because of the $8.3 billion that must come either from taxes or from increased borrowing. So the governments always can point out, "Look, we are employing 10,000 people on building this road." What is not visible is that maybe 10,000 jobs were lost in other parts of the economy.

Playing with words can be an expensive game.

NOTES

1. Canada, Parliament, House of Commons, *Debates*, Vol. 133, no. 5 (Friday, January 21, 1994) p. 138.
2. Terrance Wills, "Quebec reaches deal on federal job funds," *Ottawa Citizen*, April 12, 1997, p. A5.
3. Interview with Guy Breton was conducted in French and translated into English for use in this book.
4. House of Commons, *Debates*, Vol. 133, no. 145 (December 15, 1994) p. 9149.
5. Office of the Information Commissioner of Canada, Ruling as a Result of an Appeal to the Information Commissioner of Canada from an Unidentified Party Seeking the Short-Term Job Figures for the Canada Infrastructure Works Program [excerpt of letter]. Forwarded to Jay Innes on March 18, 1998, by Monique Leblanc-McCulloch, Treasury Board of Canada Secretariat.

6. George Anderson, Treasury Board, [letter]. Letter to Stewart Wells, assistant chief statistician of national accounts and analytical field studies, March 22, 1994.

7. George Anderson, Treasury Board, [letter]. Memo to Ottawa assistant deputy ministers, copied to federal co-chairs, March 24, 1994.

8. George Anderson, Treasury Board, [letter]. Memo to Ottawa assistant deputy ministers, copied to federal co-chairs, March 24, 1994.

9. George Anderson, Treasury Board, [letter]. Memo to Ottawa assistant deputy ministers, copied to federal co-chairs, March 24, 1994.

10. Donald Rennie, Co-ordinator, Access to Information and Privacy, Ministerial and Executive Services, Treasury Board Secretariat, [letter], June 3, 1998. Response to Access to Information request filed by Jay Innes on May 11, 1998, asking for "the actual number of jobs created by each project for Phase I and Phase II of the infrastructure program in each province and territory, and on each First Nations' reserve."

11. House of Commons, *Debates*, Vol. 133, no. 58 (April 27, 1994) p. 3571.

12. Donald Rennie, Co-ordinator, Access to Information and Privacy, Ministerial and Executive Services, [letter], June 3, 1998.

13. In response to an Access request I filed on May 11, 1998, asking how the government could be sure that the number of jobs indicated in the blue books (where projects were listed by riding) was correct, Donald Rennie wrote, "As was recently explained to you by Monique Leblanc-McCulloch of my staff, the office of infrastructure does not regularly produce a document of the actual number of jobs for Phase I and II. The reports are not machine readable. In other words, a program must be designed to generate this information. The last time such a report was produced was in the summer of 1997 in response to an ATI request made by another applicant. As this information was also provided to you in August 1997 and you have acknowledged this receipt, allow me to confirm that you hold the most recent version available." Donald Rennie, Co-ordinator, Access to Information and Privacy, Ministerial and Executive Services, [letter], June 3, 1998.

14. Office of the Auditor General of Prince Edward Island, "Chapter 6: The Infrastructure Program," *Report of the Auditor General to the Legislative Assembly, PEI, 1998* (Charlottetown: Office of the Auditor General, February 20, 1998) pp. 35–36.

15. Office of the Auditor General of Canada, "Chapter 26: Canada Infrastructure Works Program — Lessons Learned," *Report of the Auditor General of Canada, 1996* (Ottawa: Office of the Auditor General, November 1996) pp. 26–28.
16. *Report of the Auditor General of Canada, 1996*, p. 26.
17. Richard M. Soberman, *Taking Stock: A Review of the Canada Infrastructure Works Program*, Vol. 1 (Ottawa: Canada Infrastructure Works Office, Treasury Board Secretariat, August 1996), p. ii.
18. Soberman, p. x.
19. The quotations Professor Brenner refers to in the letter are taken from Richard M. Soberman, "Appendix A: Overview of Models," *Taking Stock: A Review of the Canada Infrastructure Works Program*, Vol. 2 (Ottawa: Canada Infrastructure Works Office, Treasury Board Secretariat, August 1996).

CHAPTER 16

Secrets in Low Places

Some commentators have referred to the public service as the "permanent government." Cabinet ministers and prime ministers can lose elections and political parties can fall, but the power remains with the civil servants. They are the institution's long-term memory.

In 1997 I was challenged to roll up my sleeves, get to work and prove that a citizen could make sense of government. But in a year-long effort I rarely got beyond the public servants guarding the gate.

I expected an open and transparent process with detailed records and readily available rationales explaining the reasons behind decisions. I assumed that the records kept would be pristine and detailed, if only to combat any charges of favouritism or unequal distribution of money to political parties or individual ridings. Instead I found a system shrouded in secrecy and suspicion as I uncovered problems resulting from unclear guidelines, bad choices, poor record keeping and financial mismanagement. And all the while government insisted that its method of decision making was exemplary.

While I don't intend to dwell on my frustrations and detail at length the problems with the system, there a few discoveries which randomly spring to mind whenever the team and I trace and retrace the moves we made in an attempt to gain access to information which nobody, for whatever reasons, wanted us to have.

Even *before* the federal-provincial agreements had been written, outlining the rules and the regulations of the infrastructure program, it appeared that the decision-making process was being circumvented — for example, when Liberal politicians committed infrastructure money to pay for Toronto's National Trade Centre and the Quebec City convention centre during the 1993 election campaign.

I found that the federal government had failed to enforce prudent financial policies and practices that are mandated by federal law. And no public servant would explain the reasons why the rules in the federal-provincial agreements varied between provinces.

My questions about the details of a project were often thrown from Treasury Board in Ottawa to the provincial government ministry in charge of the program, only to be answered with silence or bounced back to the federal government with a blank look and a claim that "Treasury Board should have that information." To be fair, the involvement of three levels of government forced three levels of public servants performing similar duties to try and keep track of the projects.

Deputy Prime Minister Herb Gray excused the lack of federal oversight in a speech he made in 1999: "It was a co-operative, collaborative effort built on the model of alternative service delivery. Therefore the Government of Canada felt it was not necessary to duplicate auditing and oversight efforts that the other orders of government are already conducting through their own processes."[1]

In every province we investigated there were many times when we weren't able to access the minutes of meetings where federal and provincial public servants made spending decisions to fund infrastructure projects — often because minutes had never existed.

There was no standardized project application form for the program, which may explain the sloppy record keeping that allowed information to fall through the cracks at one government level or another. To complicate matters, several public servants told us that an application could be turned down if the project could qualify for a subsidy under a different government program.

Since people in the public service are advisors to the political level, one would expect that they would have rigorously examined options and project assessments, performed cost-benefit analyses and considered the opportunity costs attached to each project. Such analyses would have helped them to defend themselves in the event that a decision to fund a community centre, bowling alley or bocce court was questioned. But, as we were told repeatedly, those tests weren't done, increasing our confusion over the selection criteria.

The auditors general of Saskatchewan, Nova Scotia and Prince Edward Island examined the program for their respective provinces, while the federal auditor general looked at the program in 1996 and again in 1999. The audits identified problems with the administration of the program, which was complicated by the various levels of government involved and the short time frames that did not allow the parties to consult before the start of the program. It appears that many of the problems originated in the planning stage, when guidelines were being drawn up to determine the ways in which the projects would be assessed and approved. With vague criteria and fluctuating rules, the public servants administering the program did not have consistent objectives to judge whether or not project applications met the goals of the program.

In response to the auditor general's 1996 report, Marcel Massé, who succeeded Art Eggleton as president of the Treasury Board and minister in charge of infrastructure, explained away the criticisms by deflecting the blame onto the public servants who administered the program: "When we are spending $6 billion on thousands and thousands of projects, it is inevitable that some projects will have been badly chosen and some of the management may have been wrong."[2]

Yet despite all the criticisms of the program, Treasury Board officials predicted an increase in cost-sharing agreements that will be modelled on the Canada Infrastructure Works Program. Paul Thibault, executive director of the Infrastructure Works Program for the Treasury Board, commented in an appearance before the Public Accounts Committee on February 20, 1997, that the "government is pleased with the program-management model developed for the Infrastructure Works Program. We intend to promote it as a model for future federal-provincial arrangements, especially where other third parties such as municipalities, colleges and universities or other private sector interests are involved in sharing costs and delivering services to the public."[3]

Toward the end of my research in Ottawa, John Williams, the Canadian Alliance MP who is the chair of the Public Accounts Committee, offered a possible explanation for the difficulties I encountered:

> Our system has become so adversarial, and because discipline is so tight, the slightest mistake is blown up into the greatest of proportions. Therefore the government will expend all efforts, regardless of the cost and benefits, to try and minimize and bring mistakes down to the barest minimum or none at all. That's why they're not interested in public policy being too well defined — because programs don't always achieve what they're designed to achieve. So if you don't set out and say, "This is what I really want to do," if you don't articulate that, then obviously the program is a success because you spent the money. That's the thing. Governments don't want to be held accountable because we set the benchmark so high that the slightest mistake is a huge embarrassment.

Was it that simple? Was the secrecy and stonewalling we had experienced from the public service the result of fear? Were the public servants worried that an unknown group of citizens could obtain information that might be used to embarrass politicians? Could that explain the ignored phone calls, censored pages and lengthy delays when responding to Access to Information requests?

One government employee offered a rare frank comment that suggested there was friction between some public servants and their political bosses. I called the Treasury Board offices for further details on the $1.3-billion program extension, and before I could even finish my question I was told that Phase II was not an extension but a "new infrastructure program" with new federal-provincial contracts. I asked, "Why, then, did the politicians refer to an 'extension' in the media?" The public servant quipped, "Because they would like you to believe that." End of conversation.

When I asked a public servant in B.C. if there was another infrastructure program on the horizon, his sarcastic reply was, "No, they haven't called an election yet."

During my investigations John Grace, who had just finished an eight-year term as the information commissioner, the official responsible for determining what information can be released to the public under Access to Information law, sat down with me at his home in Ottawa and talked about the secrecy of the public service:

> Public servants think, "It's our information." They have a proprietorial interest in the information. It's not the public servants' information. It's the people's information. The people paid for the collection. The people gave the information. And so many of these public servants say, "It's ours. Trust us."
>
> I think there is a downside to the Access law, as far as the availability of information is concerned. It's a downside that should not have occurred. But, for example, minutes of departments have been, as you found out, I think, pared down to a bare minimum because minutes by themselves should be releasable. I think this is an unfortunate byproduct of the law. It goes completely against the whole spirit of the law. But there's nothing in the law that says you must write things down.
>
> Perhaps the worst example is not simply the fact that the minutes are bare bones or worse, but people don't write things down at all. Too many senior public servants come up to me and say, "You know, John, what this law's doing, we don't write things down anymore. We wink, we nod, we speak, whatever, we just don't write it down."
>
> I think the great majority of the public servants who exempt information have good motives. They're perhaps a little timorous, but they are not evil people. It's because they've been raised in a bureaucratic culture that puts a greater value on secrecy than on openness. So they tend to give the exemptions of the [Access to Information] Act the benefit of all doubts. When in doubt, hold back; it could be kind of a motto.
>
> There is what I've called a culture of secrecy, and that's the culture that's been handed down to our rulers. Instead of a culture of openness, which I think the times demand and an educated public demands, we are really insulted by this notion of "Trust us, we know best. This information might damage the national interest. You aren't able to handle it."
>
> It's a paternalistic notion based on the preservation of power. You know, public servants, good people, most of them,

are not highly paid. People want job satisfaction, psychic satisfaction, and there's some, I suppose, satisfaction to be taken, some exclusivity, from saying, "We know this." And of course there's a common fear of embarrassment. You don't want to embarrass the minister, the government, your boss. Unfortunately, in the federal system at least, being known as a person who is open to Access requests, who believes in the concept of transparency, open government — it's not a job-enhancing position to take in government. It becomes, "Well, whose side are you on? Are you on the side of these people who want this information or are you on the side of your department who knows best? And we'll decide what goes out. We'll decide the spin."

Former P.E.I. deputy minister Andy Wells told Jennifer that during his years in government he had seen how pressures on public servants had transformed the system:

The civil service today is very politicized. As a senior public servant, you can't depend upon the new government coming in and not firing you. So there's a pretty big turnover. You have public servants looking at their jobs in the same light as a politician does. And you will find that public servants are constantly trying to please the politician rather than work the process the way it should be worked.

I'm of the old school who believed that you were in there, whether as a politician or as a public servant, to serve the public. That is your first responsibility. Unfortunately, in the last number of years I think that has turned around, and many of our political people and our senior public servant people are not doing the same kind of service for the public that I would like to see.

I used to say 30 years ago, with others, that the politician was there to establish policy. The public servant was there to recommend and respond once their decisions were made, and to implement. We constantly had to fight off politicians who wanted to do both. Well, now in many respects we have politicians and senior public servants doing both, together. Public servants are worrying about politics and the politicians are worrying about program delivery. It's a terrible situation in terms of achieving anything.

In the summer of 2000 I met Harry Swain, a former federal deputy minister with Industry Canada who was involved with the infrastructure program in Ontario. Had I met him earlier, his comments would have saved me a lot of frantic running around:

I was responsible for the delivery of that program in Ontario the first time around [Phase I], and I know that officials in Ottawa are right now spending a lot of time trying to design a better program than the one we did six years ago, which really was a mess.

One of the reasons that that program was a mess was because there was no mechanism for deciding what kinds of infrastructure were important and what were not. Was a highway more important? Was a pothole more important than a bocce court?

In fact what happened was that the decisions were left, on a highly distributive basis, to local politicians. Moreover, just to really screw up the accountability, local politicians at three levels, usually involving three different political parties that all hated each other, were all logrolling for local political advantage.

The management committee of officials simply made sure that the project was legal, not that it was optimal.

I asked Harry if the committees ever said no to a project. He replied:

Not if it was legal, and if they had the budget, and the politicians were breathing down their neck. No, never.

What that management committee body did was say, does this particular project fit within the broad eligibility criteria that had been set? And remember, I said they were very broad indeed. If it did, and if there was budget available, it was approved because it was the MLA or the alderman or the MP, whoever it was, pushing the particular project.

The politicians want to be there cutting the ribbon, they want to reward their voters, they want perhaps to influence some neighbourhood to vote more in their direction the next time, and that's why some bocce courts [were funded] versus some set of potholes. Moreover, none of this stuff is ever documented.

Here we have a program which no bureaucrat likes, which every senior official of my acquaintance has advised successive governments is a total turkey and is going to just get you in trouble, and ministers insist on going forward with it.

They distribute the decision making to MPs, MLAs and city councillors, and then they wonder why — gosh — there's no record of why a particular decision was taken. There will be a good record on what money was spent, how much that sewer cost. There will be sort of good auditable records, usually, on these things. But as to why the program was designed the way it was or why a particular decision was taken, usually there's not very much to tell you.

You could have every Access to Information request fulfilled tomorrow and it wouldn't tell you anything because the real story is not written down.

But where was the public service in this, as the body that is supposed to put forward the options and administer the program? According to Swain:

Officials did put forward advice about whether an infrastructure program made sense. Ministers then made a decision. I think accountability in this program is very clear.... What we do have, after all, is a political culture in which voters appear to be infinitely bribable. They seem to love it and governments announce infrastructure programs almost weekly.

NOTES

1. Herb Gray, Speech to the Association of Consulting Engineers of Canada [typescript copy], Ottawa, Ontario, December 2, 1999, p. 2.

2. Marcel Massé, quoted in Mark Kennedy, "Watchdog finds flaws in federal job-creation plan," *The Vancouver Sun*, November 27, 1996, p. A3.
3. Paul Thibault, Executive Director, Infrastructure Works, Secretariat of the Treasury Board of Canada. Quoted during his appearance before the Public Accounts Committee, February 20, 1997.

SECRETS IN HIGH PLACES

long-term employment. Instead we find jobs costing more than $60,000 and lasting for only a summer.

"Politics" now refers to the public's confusion when trying to figure out the reasons for bewildering government actions.

On the eve of the 2000 election the Liberals announced a new infrastructure program, even though Harry Swain's former colleagues in Ottawa warned them that the program "is a total turkey and is going to get you in trouble."

The Liberals won the election and announced a new $6 billion cost-shared program that would run until 2007 and, supposedly, help make Canada a winner in the 21st century.

In a version of political hot potato, the administration for the program bounced from Treasury Board to the office of the deputy prime minister before ending up in the hands of the minister of industry. The government flirted with the idea of giving the decision-making power to a body that is at arm's length from government, but then reversed the decision so that accountability for the program again rests in the House of Commons, on the broad and willing shoulders of our valiant members of Parliament.

And I thought to myself, "Oh, hell, I gotta go through this for another five years!!!"

CONCLUS

Since my Christmas visit to New Brunswick in 1998, when a [...]
public servant first dared whisper to me, "It's all politics," I'[...]
covered that the word "politics" has acquired a new definit[...]
Canada. That word — politics — slips easily off the tongue of so[...]
Canadians and is instantly dismissed with a wave of the hand anc[...]
of the eyes. Politics is now understood to mean a total lack of acc[...]
ability, a recognition of the fact that decisions in the political real[...]
not made in the same way as they are in the private sphere. In the[...]
ical world governments can spend billions of dollars of public n[...]
on programs such as CIWP without applying cost-benefit analyses[...]
sidering opportunity costs or even maintaining basic record kee[...]
which is often thought of as an expensive waste of resources. Mean[...]
they feed the public a constant diet of political spin in which go[...]
ment spending is called an "investment" and "improving the qual[...]
life" is the objective for a program that pays for golf greens and [...]
mowers. When it comes to job creation, images are conveyed that [...]
the impression of people in need receiving a hand up, helping them[...]

INDEX